George
Caners
99.05.25

So You Want More Money...

Here's What Works

By
George Caners
B.Sc., C.A., M.B.A., C.F.P.

Marilyn Caners – Editor
Fred Webster – Illustrator
Tom Janson – Graphics, Design, Co-Editor

Published in 1998 by Estate Services Inc.
Suite 210, 9 Broad Street
Brockville, Ontario K6V 6Z4
Telephone: 613-342-1555
Toll Free: 1-888-829-9952
Fax: 613-342-2845
e-mail: george@caners.com

Although the author has exhaustively researched all sources to ensure the accuracy and completeness of the information contained in this book, we assume no responsibility for errors, inaccuracies, omissions, or any inconsistency herein. Any slights of people or organizations are unintentional. Readers should use their own judgement and/or consult a financial expert for specific applications to their individual situations.

1st Edition, December, 1998

CANADIAN CATALOGUING IN PUBLICATION DATA

Caners, George, 1948-
    So You Want More Money – Here's What Works

ISBN 0-9684668-0-X

    1. Finance, Personal. 2. Financial security. I. Caners, Marilyn II. Title.

HG179.C286 1998   332.024'01   C98-901443-6

Printed by Henderson Printing Inc.
23 Abbott Street, Brockville, Ontario K6V 5V5

ISBN 0-9684668-0-X

9 780968 466803

Acknowledgements

Let me begin by thanking my wife, Marilyn. She was absolutely tireless in her editing from the start to the finish. She also worked diligently with me to translate the technical financial jargon into everyday language. If she did not understand something, she would not let it go until I explained the concept to her in simple English, and then she would say "why don't you say that then!"

Tom Janson did wonderful work in editing, graph design, presentation and readying the manuscript for print. He really helped give life to my ideas. Fred Webster did a superb job of capturing the essence of what I was trying to say in his cartoon drawings. But, best of all, was the final joint effort in fine-tuning put forth by Marilyn, Tom, Fred and myself. It produced a book that was far better than the sum of our individual efforts, and we had fun doing it.

I also wish to thank everyone who helped me with the book, especially those who took the time to read the manuscript and offer their suggestions. First are my three sons Chris, Jon and Kevin. Barry Raison and Jack Walker were instrumental in putting the original manuscript into readable form. However, there were many other people who contributed their ideas. Here are some I wish to specifically thank: David Beatty, Gordon Burgess, Dennis and Deb Caners, Maureen Crawford, Laurence Croswell, Joy Goodfellow, Doug Hale, Sue Janson, Cynthia Kall, Jim Little, Bob Lucey, Tony Maneely, Chris Punnett, Lisa Punnett, Lisa Raymond and Brian Tuthill. I needed your encouragement and ideas to keep going.

I especially wish to thank my many clients, who shared with me their practical experience and wisdom. This book would not have been possible without you.

SO YOU WANT MORE MONEY – HERE'S WHAT WORKS

Chapter 1

Introduction

So you want more money? This book will show you what works.

I am an accountant with my own public practice. A major part of my work involves completing personal tax returns and doing financial planning. Over the years, I realized that there was a common pattern in the methods used by people who had dramatically increased their wealth. I combined my financial knowledge with my clients' practical experiences to develop my investment strategy. The result was that my own investments grew at a rate I thought was impossible. In retrospect, it was not by chance that this happened. I put myself in a position to take advantage of the opportunities as they presented themselves. The outcome was almost inevitable.

There is no doubt that the lack of personal financial security causes immense anxiety in many people. However, one wealthy person I know said, "There is nothing easier than making money". This is a bit of an overstatement, but I hear what he is saying. So, if it is so easy to make money, why are so many people having such problems? How can such a contradiction exist? The answer lies in the way people approach investing.

One event, more than any other, helped twig my curiosity in the area of wealth creation. I did financial work for two people who worked for the same company. They both had a university degree, were married, had children, and were the same age. Even though their incomes were somewhat different, people would have assumed that they had comparable wealth. However, one had 100 times more money than the other! Why? The answer was that they had used very different financial strategies. In the long run, using the correct approach has a tremendous impact on your wealth.

There is a key characteristic shared by people such as Warren Buffett and Peter Lynch (two very successful investors). It is their ability to frequently challenge and revise their own assumptions and opinions about investing. They are very open to new ways of improving their investment returns. Also, they do not dwell on mistakes. They learn from them and keep going. Since they were so successful, it makes sense for us to copy their methods until we learn better ones ourselves. Although it requires courage and self-confidence, be open to new ideas. The effort is worth it.

There are three critically important elements necessary in order to grow your money. The first and foremost of these is desire, which must come from you. Without a strong, consistent desire, nothing will happen. The other two elements are a solid knowledge about investments, and adequate skills to implement this knowledge. This book will provide you with excellent knowledge. You will develop the required skills by applying this knowledge. It is only when all three elements work together (overlap) that success is yours. As the area of overlap increases, so will your wealth.

The following diagram illustrates this concept.

Success in Creating Wealth

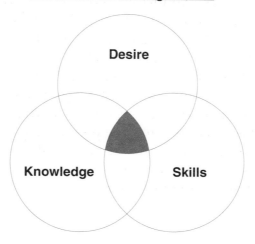

Desire

Knowledge   **Skills**

Successful investment is a race against time. No matter how good you are at investing, you still need money to start, and time for it to grow. The less money you have to begin with, the more growth time is required. A good analogy is in growing a tree. First you need the seedling, and then you need time. The amount of time required for growth can be discouraging. However, never forget that the best time to plant an oak tree was 50 years ago - the next best time is right now. The same holds true with investments.

At this point, I want to introduce you to a friend of mine, the '$6.50 a day man'. You may have already noticed him on the first page of this chapter. He will appear at the start of each chapter. His movement from one chapter to the next represents one year in his life.

He was broke at the start of this chapter. However, he had started to take control of his financial situation by saving $6.50 per day. Now, at the end of his first year, he has saved $2,373. (I will round this to $2,370 for simplicity.) By buying an RRSP and using the tax saving, he consequently has $4,000, which is invested at 10%. (As will be discussed later, I feel that this rate is attainable.) He will continue to save and invest at the same rate throughout the book.

At the beginning of each chapter, you will see how his fortune has progressed from the previous year. I think you will be amazed at how well he does. In the appendix, he appears as a retired man, to show you how much money he has accumulated over forty years.

Chapter 2

Drift, Drown or Decide

Y ou are faced with three choices in financial planning, just as you are in other areas of life. You can drift, drown or decide.

The 'drifter' sees himself as a small boat on the huge ocean of life. The wind and the waves are the primary determinates of where he ends up, as he drifts along with no plans.

DRIFT

Eventually, he will reach the shore. A drifter feels life is not easy, but not bad either. The typical drifter lives in a house or condo. There is enough to get by on, but he cannot afford many luxuries. He doesn't understand finances very well. His retirement planning is minimal. It hardly occurs to him to put pen to paper, and figure it out ahead of time.

The 'drowner' finds life a continuous struggle. It is not a matter of picking a shore to land on, but rather a case of managing to stay above the next wave as his boat is buffeted by gale force winds.

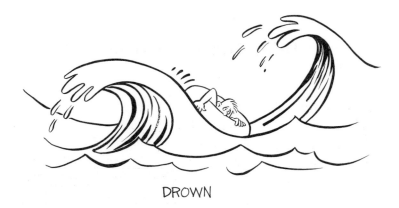

DROWN

He tires of trying to survive the many short-term crises that arise, one after another. The drowner ends up in a small apartment, barely making ends meet. Life is tough, and he blames others for his misfortune. Retirement planning is non-existent.

The 'decider' sees the shore and realizes that safety and the good life beckon her. The task becomes one of choosing which shore, and then where to land on that shore. She assesses her options, makes choices and acts on them.

DECIDE

Abundance is there for the taking. The decider intuitively knows the easiest way to predict the future is to make it happen. She often puts pen to paper to see if she will have enough money to meet her needs. She has a lovely house at the edge of a lake.

I know someone who has taken the decider concept to the extreme. He has researched various places around the world where he may want to retire, and the annual cost of doing so at each location. He has done a remarkable amount of detailed analysis, right down to the cost of the maid and groundskeeper! He has worked out all these options so that he knows what he can afford at various levels of income. Obviously, most of us will not go to this length, nor should we.

In my public practice, I see many people drifting – letting events control them instead of taking charge themselves. I also see a small number of people drowning. Usually these drowners are unaware that they are contributing to their own demise. I also see deciders. No matter what their situation, they feel they can exert control.

It takes just a tiny change in attitude for a drifter or drowner to become a decider. Once you become a decider, a positive outcome is certain.

Chapter 3

The Basics

The reason we want more money is so that we can do whatever we want, whenever we want. Once you start saving, you'll discover the magic of capital: your money working for you all the time, even as you sleep. Save money and invest it wisely; over time, this capital will earn more for you than you earn from your job. At this point, you have achieved financial independence. What amazes me is how little you have to save to make this happen. However, the savings must start as soon as possible, and must be continued until your goal is reached. It's like walking toward a destination. You'll get there, provided you keep moving in the right direction.

Your success in reaching financial independence depends upon three key steps. First, determine what the goal is. How much money do you really want, and when do you want to have it? Next, establish a logical plan to reach this goal in the time provided. Finally, you must have a feedback system to monitor your progress. If your monitoring system finds that you aren't achieving your goal, change your plan. A feedback system is meaningless if it does not encourage you to take action when warranted.

The first of these steps, determining your goal, is by far the most important. It is not enough to think a goal is possible. We must <u>know</u> we will reach financial independence, as opposed to just dreaming about it. We must be a decider. The only uncertainty is when we will reach the goal, not if we will reach it.

1. Your Goal

Most people require the money earned from a job to pay for their expenditures. The real purpose of wealth creation is to do away with the need to have a job. Your choosing to retire is only possible when your capital (money saved) generates enough cash to meet or exceed your expenditures. It is only when you reach this point that work becomes a choice, rather than a necessity. There is nothing that reduces work stress as much as the knowledge that you do not need the job.

Therefore, your goal becomes one of having sufficient savings to generate all the money that you require in order to do the things you want. Your plan will have an impact on how quickly you can accomplish this goal, and what lifestyle you can afford. Once you no longer need to work, you may have further goals for which you must save. For example, you may wish to leave a legacy to your children, or fund a charitable cause to help those in need.

How much money do you need? It depends. Let me give you the extremes I have witnessed. Early on in my practice, a woman in her late 60's walked into my office and asked me to do her tax return, and her husband's. They had no investments whatsoever. Their only sources of income were the Canada Pension Plan (CPP) and Old Age Security (OAS). Their combined annual income was about $16,000. What I really found surprising was that they had given more than $2,000 to charity! I explained to her that they had no taxes to pay, and consequently their charitable receipts would provide them with no taxable benefit. She didn't care. There was a warm glow about this lady. She felt extremely lucky that they could give $2,000 to help others. They had no savings, and yet they appeared to have no need for any. This couple was able to live comfortably on less than their $16,000 income. This was a remarkable woman. I will never forget her. She was the 'richest' person I have ever met. She felt abundance. In my opinion, this feeling of abundance is the only true measure of wealth. It has nothing to do with how much money you have in the bank.

On the other side of the spectrum is another client I greatly respect. Before retiring, he believes he should own his house outright, and have at least $3 million in liquid assets (money in the bank, GICs, stocks and bonds). One million is to provide an income stream, one million is to buy toys he so desires, and the third million is his safety net. He has achieved this, and is still working to accumulate more wealth. Most would consider his requirements excessive. You are likely to find your capital needs somewhere between these two extremes of zero and $3 million!

To answer the question of how much money you need to 'retire', (meaning work is not necessary for income), try the three-quarters rule. Retired people spend about three-quarters of what they used to spend while they were

YOUR GOAL

working. Examine what you are spending now. Take three-quarters of that amount, and make adjustments for changes in your lifestyle. For example, if you plan to travel extensively during your retirement, you may need more money than you did while working. On the other hand, if you prefer to sit back and take it easy, then your requirements will be much less than when you were working. Therefore, it is important for you to first determine what your plans are before applying the three-quarters rule.

There is another fact to consider. Many of the basic necessities of life, e.g. apples, oranges, tissue, soap, etc., cost the same to all people, whether they are rich or poor. Someone at a lower-income level may require more than three-quarters of pre-retirement income to live comfortably. Someone with a higher income would require less than three-quarters to do the same. For example, someone earning $20,000 while working may have difficulty living on $15,000 (75% of $20,000). However, someone earning $60,000 while working would probably require less than $45,000 (75% of $60,000).

Remember that so far all you have calculated is the amount of money you need. You require enough savings to generate this income. Over the past 48 years (1950 - 1997), savings invested in five-year term deposits have provided an average rate of return (interest earned) of 8%[1]. At this rate, you would require about $100,000 of savings to produce each $8,000 of annual revenue. You could also spend some of this $100,000. But you would then be left with less money to generate future income, so be careful. Now you can see why you need to start saving early. It takes a lot of money to generate enough wealth to live comfortably. To determine how much investment is required to support expenses, I use a much more sophisticated calculation for my clients. It considers the rate of return expected from their savings, when they plan to stop working, inflation, and taxes. However, the above rule of thumb is much easier to understand and puts you in the ballpark.

One investor friend of mine feels you shouldn't even count on earning 8% annually. He believes you should only expect an annual rate of return of between 5% to 6.7%. In other words, you would have to save $120,000 to $160,000 to generate $8,000 annually. An easier way of remembering

---

[1] 1997 Andex Chart for Canadian Investors, Andex Associates Inc.

this is that you would need to save 15 to 20 times more than the amount of income you want generated.

One of the realities of life is inflation. It averaged 4.3% in the past 48 years.[2] At this rate, your money loses half of its value every 17 years. Therefore, every $1,000 of savings at retirement (age 50) will be worth only $500 at age 67, and only $250 at age 84.

Please note that all tables and charts in this book are not adjusted for inflation, with the exception of one in Chapter 8, "Risk".

After you have determined the amount of income you wish to have, the next step is to calculate how much you can expect from all sources other than investments. For example, will you receive money from the Canada Pension Plan? If so, how much? This is easy to find out. Simply write to the Health and Welfare Canada office in your area. The address can be found in your local telephone book under the federal government listings. In 1997, the maximum annual payment from CPP was $8,842. The CPP will vary depending on how much you paid into it (based on your pre-retirement earnings) and on whether or not you decide to start drawing it early. Another source of income is Old Age Security (1997 annual maximum was $4,847). OAS is dependent upon income, and currently starts after you turn 65. The federal government is presently revamping the retirement income system, so be conservative when calculating how much you can expect from this source.

You may also have a company pension plan. It is very possible that with a generous pension plan, you will be able to enjoy a good retirement, without the need for any other savings. If you don't have a pension, you must rely on your own Registered Retirement Savings Plan (RRSP), and other savings. (RRSPs are covered in detail in Chapter 10). Let's

---

[2] 1997 Andex Chart for Canadian Investors, Andex Associates Inc.

look at the statistics. Fewer than half of Canadians, age 50 and under, even have a company pension plan.[3] Some plans, such as teachers' pension plans, have high premiums (what employees pay in), and provide a handsome pay-off, which is indexed to inflation. An example of a generous pension plan is the one paid to Federal and Provincial politicians. Far behind, but still excellent, are civil servant and public sector pension plans. Very few private sector plans are as good. The reason is obvious. These plans are a significant cost to the employer, whose first goal is to protect the bottom line and make a dollar.

Canadians can contribute up to 18% of their previous year's earned income to an RRSP (annual maximum $13,500). Revenue Canada has a specific definition for earned income. For most people, earned income is the amount made from employment. Someone who always invests the maximum allowed in RRSPs, and works to age 65, will probably not have a shortage of money during retirement. However, you may find yourself struggling in later years, if you have not been contributing the yearly maximum, or close to it. What is your situation?

If you do have a company pension plan, it reduces the amount you are allowed to tax shelter (defer from tax) in an RRSP. Don't worry about this. Your employer has put money aside for you in a pension plan, and that is why your RRSP limit has been reduced. The combined company pension, plus the amount you put away in an RRSP, should provide the same tax benefit as if you contributed the entire amount to an RRSP. If you are not using all of your RRSP 'room', (the cumulative total of yearly contributions that you are allowed to make), your financial goal may be too low. Start rectifying the situation now by filling up the unused RRSP room. Buying RRSPs and paying down debt

---

[3] The Globe and Mail.

are the two best strategies to provide you with more money in the future.

Bear with me while we look at some numbers. Suppose that in your five final years of work you earned $36,000, $37,000, $38,000, $39,000, and $40,000 respectively. Company pensions are often based on an employee's best five years. We will assume the five highest-paid years were also the five final years – in this case, an average income of $38,000. Now assume that the pension for this employee would be 70% of $38,000 or $26,600 annually. Most pension plans allow the pensioner to elect a continuity option, which decreases the pension while the pensioner is still alive, but continues to pay the deceased person's spouse. In this example, the spouse would receive 60% of $26,600 or $15,960 annually after the pensioner dies. (With 4.3% inflation, this $15,960 pension will be worth about $8,000 annually in 17 years and $4,000 in 34 years.) What looks adequate today might not amount to very much in a few years from now.

With pensions, the surviving spouse may be left destitute if the correct choice (continuity option) has not been made when the pension was set up. On the other hand, RRSPs do not vanish with the death of the person who holds them. The balance is usually passed tax-free to the spouse. If there is no spouse, or if the RRSP funds are willed to someone else, then upon death this tax-sheltered money is brought into income, taxes are paid on it, and the balance is given to the estate.

Err on the side of caution. Start saving now. I have yet to hear a single person complain because he or she has saved too much. We all know people who are in their eighties and nineties. A significant portion of your life will be spent in retirement. It makes good sense to begin preparing early for what will hopefully be a lengthy retirement period.

Right now, grab a pen and a piece of paper. How much more money do you need to save before you have the option of retiring? How many years will it take to get there at your current savings rate? Are you happy with this? What, if anything, are you going to do about it?

Don't start reading again until you have calculated how much you need to retire in the lifestyle of your choice. Remember, it is better to be vaguely right than precisely wrong - you will be wrong if you don't even bother to calculate this number.

2. Your Plan

You now know how much money you want. You also know what to expect as income from CPP, OAS, and pension plans. Income generated from your RRSPs and other investments must make up any shortfall.

There are two important steps to every financial plan. The first step is that you must save a certain amount each year. My father's favorite saying on this subject was, "You can't save water in a leaky bucket". Plug the holes (expenditures) and there will be water (money) when you need it. This action in itself almost guarantees your success in saving. The second step is that you must have a sound strategy to grow these savings.

LEAKY SAVINGS BUCKET

The best strategy to make savings grow is to use an RRSP. (It is discussed in detail in Chapter 10, "RRSPs".) The following graph shows the results of implementing this strategy. I used $4,000 as the amount invested, as that was the average 1995 Canadian RRSP contribution.[4] I have used a 10% rate of return for a reason. It's between the rate of return earned by 5 year GICs (8%) and that of Canadian stocks (11%) from 1950 - 1997.

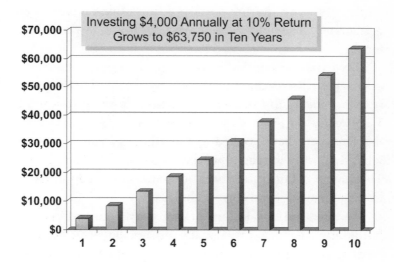

The graph shows that $4,000 invested annually in an RRSP at an arbitrary growth rate of 10%, for a 10-year period, grows to $63,750! Can you save $ 6.50 per day ($2,370 annually)? That is all you need to generate the $4,000 to invest in the RRSP.[5]

3. Your Feedback System

I have noticed that successful investors carefully monitor their investment results. They have a feedback system that is accurate, organized, and simple. Investors who are not as successful generally lack this tool.

---

[4] The Globe and Mail December 7, 1995.

[5] A $4,000 RRSP investment provides $1,640 in tax savings. Therefore $2,370 is in fact $10 more than the actual amount of money that you need to add to the tax savings to buy a $4,000 RRSP.

Using Accurate Information

Occasionally my father used to play poker with five friends. It always amused him that when the players around the table at evening's end shared how well they had done, the total money won was always greater than the total money lost! This doesn't add up. I don't think anyone lied deliberately. They just didn't have an accurate feedback system.

My experience is that most people exaggerate their success when discussing their stock market and investment results, too. Again, this embellishment is rarely deceitful. They really do think they have done very well. However, they may not have looked at the whole picture. They see what they want to see, rather than what is really happening. They have a faulty feedback system, which continues to lead them away from correct choices.

People who buy lottery tickets, play a lot of bingo, or frequently visit casinos, usually do not have an accurate feedback system. If they did have one, I think they would be discouraged from gambling (assuming that they were not suffering from an addiction to it). Without correct information, we are in the same position as our ancestors who believed that the earth was the centre of the universe. Galileo, with accurate data, calculated that it would be impossible for the sun to revolve around the earth. His feedback system changed his thinking, and the world's.

An effective feedback system is absolutely essential as a basis for making logical investment decisions.

Getting Organized

Let's talk about what else makes a good feedback system. First, your information should be easily retrieved. (A friend of mine used to say, "I have an excellent filing system. It is my retrieval system that stinks!") We can waste a lot of time looking for things. A little bit of organization can be very helpful. I am not the world's most organized person, but I have learned a lot from those around me.

If you are sufficiently organized to do something right the first time, you will not have to take time to do it over. Here is my favorite example. I had arranged a family trip to Toronto to see a baseball game. After driving one hour, I suddenly realized that our baseball tickets were still at home! Back we went. We wasted two hours. It would have taken only seconds for me to check if I had the tickets prior to leaving. A list or some other method of organizing myself would have eliminated this problem.

My wife, Marilyn, is highly organized. She arranges things in a way that makes forgetting almost impossible. For example, in the case of the baseball tickets, she would have put them in her purse the night before we left. If she has to return something to a store, she will put the item in the front seat of her car. The item is returned the next time that the car is used. If she has to pick up an item, she will remind herself with a note attached to the center of her car's steering wheel.

Being organized will help you develop a good feedback system. Start by having all your financial records in only one place. I recommend that you purchase a two-drawer filing cabinet. One drawer is for your permanent files -- those items that you are finished with, but want to keep. Examples of these include your old bank statements, tax returns with attached receipts, contracts, and legal documents. Make sure that each document is in a properly labeled file. We use manila file folders, and fasten the documents inside with a two-hole punch system. Fastened documents don't get lost.

The other drawer is used for more current documents. Examples of these include recent bank statements, utility bills, and statements for credit cards and investments. In this drawer, we also have a big envelope marked "Taxes" in which we put all receipts required to file next year's tax return e.g. RRSPs, charitable donations, T-4 and T-5 slips, tuition receipts, etc. This system works well for us. We can put our hands on any of this information in a matter of minutes.

Keeping It Simple - Cash

The best method I have found to track cash came from my university roommate. He would start each week by recording (in a small notebook) the amount of paper money in his wallet. Whenever he bought something, he would record only the paper money spent, and ignore the coin. For instance, if he bought a cup of coffee for $1.50 with a $10 bill, he would get back a $5 bill and $3.50 in coin. Five dollars of paper money would now be gone. This would therefore be recorded as "coffee – $5.00", and would be subtracted from his starting amount. If later in the day, he bought another coffee and this time spent only coin on it, he would not record it. At the end of the week, he would compare what paper money he had left in his wallet to the amount left according to his notebook. If the two figures didn't agree, it either meant he forgot to record something, or he had lost some money.

I use my roommate's system to this day. The notebook is kept in my top desk drawer at work. It takes me only a few minutes, a couple of times a week, to record where money was spent. Once a month, I take five minutes to total the expenditures, accounting for which of my out-of-pocket expenses relate to my business. It's the type of workload I can handle.

Keeping It Simple - Banking

Marilyn and I have just one joint chequing account, which forms the heart of our feedback system. Marilyn maintains a running bank balance by recording all deposits to, or withdrawals from, this account. To do this she carries a chequebook in her purse. Not only does she record withdrawals such as cheques written, she also records each time she uses her debit card. Therefore, we always know how much money is in the bank.

We usually try to pay the bills the same day they arrive in the mail. We do this for several reasons. First, we hate owing money. Second, the bill is handled and out of the way. Third, the people that we deal with appreciate quick payment. Finally, when our bank account goes down, we are less tempted to spend money.

We put most recurring bills, such as Ontario Hydro, on automatic bank debit. My job is reduced to just updating the chequebook record, when notices of these bills arrive. I like this, because there is less work to do than writing cheques.

When we receive our bank statement, I do a bank reconciliation (compare it to Marilyn's chequebook record). For every transaction that I confirm on the bank statement and then tick off, I also tick it off in the chequebook. I then add up the cheques that have been written, but haven't yet cleared the bank (i.e. the ones in the chequebook with no

ticks beside them). I round off the cents to the next highest dollar. I subtract this amount from the closing balance on the bank statement. This balance is what the running bank balance should be in our chequebook record. If the chequebook record is in error, it is adjusted to what the correct balance should be. This method also catches anything that has passed through our account that does not belong to us. It is best if both partners understand the entire process, so that either of you can do it.

Many people spend a lot of time finding where they have made addition and/or subtraction errors in their own chequebook record. I don't. I trust the bank's computers to accurately do this task for me. My bank reconciliation never takes me more than 15 minutes. It pays to keep things simple, because then they get done.

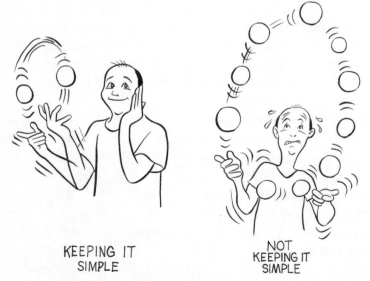

KEEPING IT
SIMPLE

NOT
KEEPING IT
SIMPLE

I knew one couple who had six bank accounts: hers, his, joint, rent, insurance, and savings. They were always transferring money from one account to another to cover cash shortfalls. All this complexity did not add to their wealth –

it just added to their work. It is much easier to juggle two balls in the air, rather than three or more balls. Similarly, the key to a good feedback system is to keep it simple, so that attention will be focused on important matters.

Keeping It Simple - Credit Cards

I have only one credit card and I use it for most of my purchases. I do this because it is very handy, and it provides me with a record of what I bought. The credit card statement becomes my feedback system.

Every time the credit card is used, the receipt goes in my wallet. Once or twice a week, I record the amounts in a notebook, and put the receipts in an envelope. This envelope and notebook are also kept in my top desk drawer at work. Each month is kept in a separate envelope, marked accordingly. This system takes very little time, and provides valuable information. It tracks what I am spending my money on, and gives me a record to check against my credit card statement.

I know my credit card balance at any time. I don't need the bank to tell me this. I am in charge. There is another big advantage to my system. Because I am always aware of what I owe, I'm less likely to spend recklessly.

I do not know why anyone would want more than one credit card. However, one credit counselor told me that one of his clients had thirty-eight credit cards! Did you realize that was even possible? There are no rewards for complexity. I can guarantee that this consumer had no idea of the outstanding credit card balances.

It is a good idea, however, for a husband and wife to have separate credit and debit cards from each other. I have heard stories of a widow's credit card being cancelled when her husband died, because her card was held jointly with his. There is another reason why my wife and I have separate cards. Once when we were at a restaurant in California, my credit card wouldn't work for some reason. Hers did.

Keeping It Simple - Investments

My wife and I each have one self-administered RRSP account. Also, we jointly have just one investment account at a brokerage house (a corporation that specializes in buying and selling stocks, bonds etc.). This means that between the two of us we receive just one T-5 slip, which is the tax slip reporting interest and dividend income. Note how simple this makes our tax returns.

The investments within our RRSPs and joint investment account are solely in company shares, and at that, are only in eleven different companies. Occasionally, I buy more shares of these companies when I have spare cash. I rarely sell. My goal is to accumulate shares, not trade them. To make matters even simpler, I try to buy shares in even numbers. For example, I may buy 100, 200, 500 or 1,000 shares of a company, not 223. This makes it very easy to recall what I own. (I will be going into detail about share ownership in future chapters.)

On January 1st of each year, I record the market value of our investment account, which includes the shares and any cash not yet invested. I keep track of any additional money put into the account at any time. The January 1st amount, plus any additions, becomes my new base amount. Once a month, my broker sends me an account statement, which details the shares and cash held to date. After verifying its accuracy, I compare the account's current total value per the statement, to my base amount. I then calculate the amount and percentage earned or lost from the start of the year. This percentage figure is my average rate of return. I record these numbers on the statements, which I keep in a binder. I like to compare my rate of return to the market average (for example, the Toronto 35 index that is explained later). I feel that I am only doing well to the extent that this benchmark is exceeded.

I summarize performance on a yearly basis, and decide if I should make any changes. The question that I always ask myself is why not sell my least favorite stock and buy more of my favorite one? To date, being too diversified has been my biggest error.

Many people use their computer to keep track of their investments. Be mindful that if you are very dependent on your computer for feedback, it may be an indication that your investments are too complicated.

The Internet is a wonderful tool to use in checking the current value of your shares. Remember, though, that your investments are long term. Don't be enticed to trade by watching the daily share value rise and fall.

Is Your Feedback System Working? - If Not, Take Action

Let's stop and do a test of your feedback system. Do you know how much money is in your wallet right now? Anyone who is careful with his or her money, and is organized, would know the correct amount. Do you know exactly how much money is in your bank account? How many cheques have you written that have not yet cleared? Do you keep your bank machine withdrawal slips until you have updated your records? Do you know the up-to-date outstanding balance on your credit card? In other words, what would you owe if you were to pay off your credit card in full today? Finally, do you know the total balance of your investments as of the end of last month?

If you don't know the above amounts, or cannot obtain these numbers quickly from your own records, you need to modify your feedback system. Remember that you can't save water in a leaky pail. Without accurate feedback, you don't know if your pail is leaking, or if it even has a bottom!

It has been my experience that the more wealth someone has, the easier they can answer the above questions. Money is important to them, and they know where they spend it. They are in control. With accurate feedback, they can draw valid conclusions and constantly fine-tune their strategy. On the other hand, people with little money are not in control. Their feedback system is rotten. They spend without being fully aware of how they stand financially. It is no accident that those with a poor feedback system often have the least wealth.

Summary

Growing wealth is similar to filling a bucket with water. Step one is deciding how much water you want (i.e. your goal). Step two is plugging all the holes in the bucket, so that you can start collecting the water (i.e. your plan). Step three is checking the bucket every once in a while to see how high the water is. If you suspect that some water is leaking out, carefully inspect the bucket and patch the leaks (feedback and action).

Chapter 4

Save Before Spending

"The success or failure of a long range savings and investment plan is not predicated on the rate of return. Its success depends on the use of a systematic plan of putting money in and leaving it there."
        - internationally famous financier Bernard M. Baruch

The prerequisite for saving is learning to spend less than you earn. This action will free up some money which, if invested wisely, will grow rapidly. The amount saved, plus its growth, must be sufficient to meet your future monetary needs.

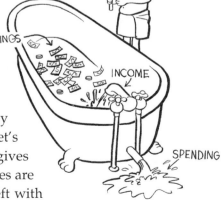

Your savings can be analogous to water in a bathtub. The water coming through the faucet represents your income, the drain represents your spending. You will be left high and dry with no savings, unless the inflow exceeds the outflow.

The following point may encourage you to save. Let's suppose your employer gives you a $2,000 raise. After taxes are paid on it, you would be left with about $1,000. Another way to have an extra $1,000 would be to cut back on your expenditures by the same amount. Therefore, every time you manage to save some money, imagine that your boss just gave you a pay raise of twice that amount. You will be very pleased with yourself!

Spending habits are the real culprits that interfere with saving money. Most of your spending is done subconsciously, and therefore you are not even aware of what is happening. If you, like most people, want to save more money, you must examine your spending habits, and stop the ones that are not serving you well. I have read that it takes just 21 days to create a new habit.[6] So, in just three weeks, you could learn to start saving before spending.

Let's examine how you spend your money. The three categories consist of an expense, a depreciating asset, and an appreciating asset:

1. An expense is an item or activity where, once the money is paid out, it is gone. None of it can be recaptured. A large portion of your money goes towards expenses, which include things such as living costs, entertainment, holidays and dining out.

2. A depreciating asset loses value over time. The longer it is held, the less valuable the item becomes. Examples include your car, furniture, computer, and stereo system.

3. An appreciating asset is something that we expect will increase in value as time passes. Examples include stocks, antiques, savings bonds, home and property.

It is important to note that if you want your wealth to grow, you have to spend less on expenses, and more on appreciating assets. You must realize that you have these choices.

---

[6] "The 7 Habits of Highly Effective People", Stephen R. Covey.

I have a friend who has a very different way of looking at what most people call assets e.g. car, cottage, and boat. He believes that all these things are actually liabilities i.e. they consume cash, not generate it. To become wealthy, he feels we must reverse our thinking about what constitutes a real asset.

One of the cardinal rules of financial planning is that it is never wise to borrow money for an expense. Instead, save for it. When you incur that expense e.g. a dream vacation, you will really enjoy it because of the planning that has gone into it, and because you won't have to continue paying for it long after it is over. Be in control. Financial pressure causes a great deal of stress to many people. I believe that by saving before spending, a lot of financial worries could be alleviated.

Credit cards are handy to use, but be aware that they do encourage you to spend more. Local merchants tell me that there is no doubt that their customers are not as price sensitive when they use a credit card instead of cash. The convenience of plastic also makes impulse buying much easier.

A credit card company earns its money by collecting, from the merchant, a percentage of the sales paid for by credit card. The more consumers use credit cards, the more credit card companies make. Therefore, they offer incentives to encourage use of their card. One example of such an incentive is air miles. For every dollar you spend with your card, you receive one air mile. It requires 15,000 air miles to fly from Toronto to Winnipeg, a trip that costs about $340.[7] This is not a huge reward for $15,000 worth of spending. It works out to be only 2.3% ($340 ÷ $15,000). Be very careful that these incentives do not entice you to spend more.

You must never pay interest on credit cards. If you do, it is almost a sure sign of financial mismanagement (your expenses exceed your income). Over 60% of Canadians do not pay off the full balance on their credit cards every month![8] If this is your situation, strong action must be taken. Perhaps the card should be cut up. I knew one couple who froze their credit card in a block of ice. Apparently, the only way to get at the card without wrecking it was to let the ice melt, allowing them to seriously rethink their spending. This measure worked for them. It is no small feat to bring your spending under control. Change the habit of using your credit card to one of using cash instead. This one change may lead you toward financial freedom.

In general, there is a pattern in how much you spend and save at various stages of your life.[9] There are three phases when spending is high. The first one occurs concurrently with the birth of your children. The home is bought and filled with furniture and kids. The second phase is when the children leave home to start post-secondary education or similar endeavors. This is a stage I am just starting

---

[7] Canadian Airlines Ticketing Centre.
[8] Royal Bank Visa Centre, October 1998.
[9] "Boom, Bust & Echo, How to Profit from the Coming Demographic Shift", David K. Foot with Daniel Stoffman.

to experience. The third phase starts at age 60-65 as retirement commences. The income from employment stops, and the amount of cash coming in sharply decreases.

The in-between phases are when you will be able to contribute the most to your savings. The first phase is after the furniture has been bought, the children are too young to drain off money for post secondary education, and the mortgage is nearly paid off. The second saving phase is when the children have left home, but you have not yet retired.

Regardless of the stage you are in, saving some money is very important. Remember, it is akin to cultivating a forest. If you fail to plant seedlings, there will never be trees to harvest. This point cannot be overemphasized. There is no magic. The only way to acquire seedlings in the first place is to follow the 'save before spending' rule. You must resist the lure of advertising that encourages you to spend every cent you make. Instead, choose to first save a portion from each paycheque, and then spend the rest only as required. This approach is often referred to as 'paying yourself first'.

One method to save before spending is to make arrangements with your employer for a pre-authorized payroll deduction, whereby a predetermined amount of money is deducted from your cheque, and deposited directly into your investment account. On the other hand, you may have already arranged for your entire paycheque to be automatically deposited into your chequing account. In that case, you can ask your banker or stockbroker to regularly withdraw money from that account, for deposit into an investment account. Your nest egg will be accumulating without you even lifting a finger. Many people find they do not miss money that they have never seen in the first place.

Consider the following two examples. I know a fellow who typically spends every dollar he earns. He gets excited about all the money he saves by finding good deals. For instance, he tells me how much he saves by driving 100 km to the nearest warehouse outlet. This man has no investments put aside for his future, but is overflowing with ideas of how to 'save' money. The problem is that all his 'savings' involve spending more money. Another person I know always has his employer deduct more income tax than is necessary. At tax time, he receives a sizable refund. Every year this refund is used to buy next year's RRSPs. He has learned to save before spending.

Many of the 'save before spending' plans may not appear to make a lot of sense. You may wonder why you should let Revenue Canada have your money interest free, when you could invest it and have this money working for you. However, human nature being what it is, we tend to spend whatever money is available. In other words, this method may not be perfect, but at least it guarantees that money is saved.

Budgeting may help some people save, although from my observations, budgets are seldom successful. They are too inflexible to meet the rapidly changing lifestyle of the modern family. If you can budget effectively, by all means, do it. On the other hand, if you can't, don't feel guilty. You have lots of company - about 95% of the population.

How do I personally save before spending? I invest the maximum allowable in RRSPs, and do so as soon as I can. In other words, I buy my RRSPs on January 2nd of the year to which the tax savings will apply, instead of waiting for the final deadline of February 28th of the next year. I feel committed to doing this, so I save all year for it. If I don't have all the money by January 2nd, I still buy all my RRSPs by borrowing the balance. I pay off this loan as soon as possible. (I will not borrow to buy RRSPs unless I feel confident that the loan will be paid off within one year.)

When I can manage it, I put any extra cash I have into investments outside my RRSPs. Once the money is invested, I am steadfast in keeping it there. If I need money to cover an unexpected cash flow, I would sooner take out a short-term loan than cash in these investments. This saving system is not very fancy, but it works for me. Does your system work for you?

John Templeton is one of the great investors of our time. He is a firm advocate of the 'save before spending' principle. In his autobiography, he mentions that he and his wife worked very hard to save half of what they earned! This process began as soon as they were married. I am not suggesting that you do this. However, is it any wonder that today John Templeton and his wife are very wealthy? Using the analogy of tree planting, it is obvious that Mr. Templeton recognized the value of planting a very large number of young trees as early as he could. He also had the wisdom to plant them in places where they grew very quickly.

Chapter 5

Examine Your Needs

"Advertising may be described as the science of arresting the human intelligence long enough to get money from it."

-Stephen Leacock

Ibelieve our needs are unique to each of us. For instance, some people have a very strong desire to buy every new gadget that comes on the market, while others do not. Take the example of someone who is content with a rotary dial phone, while another must have a cell phone, or features such as call waiting. The more you want these things, the more control you require to stop yourself from spending. This is no different from other areas of your life. If you love sweets, and have a weight problem, it may be in your best interest to keep pastries out of the house.

The secret to business success is to create a strong need, and then satisfy this need in exchange for a customer's money. Remember the cabbage patch doll craze? People wanted these dolls so desperately that a person was actually trampled to death in the scramble to get one!

The secret to our personal success, however, as taught by many gurus, is to have as few needs as possible. Happiness is an internal state of mind. Pursuing happiness by satisfying only external desires (material items) leads nowhere in the end.

Confucius say :
The contented person
is never poor.

Limiting your needs is especially important as you start to build your saving base. Once your investments really start to grow, they will increase so rapidly that you will be able to afford almost anything you want. At this point, you will not have to restrain yourself from buying.

Let me tell you about a man that I know who limits his needs. He and I were with a group of 40 other men, on a two-day ski trip to Mount Tremblant, Quebec. A major ski manufacturer was offering free product trials for their new 'carving skis'. These skis are supposed to help a good skier look like an expert. I asked my buddy if he was going to try these new skis. "No," he said. I was surprised because, in my opinion he is a pretty good skier, and I thought he would be interested in testing these new skis, especially since there was no cost involved.

He then explained his rationale. He was not in the market for new skis. If he tried the new skis and found he did not like them, he had just wasted a bit of time. On the other hand, if the new skis were a little better than his current ones, all he accomplished was to create a need that currently didn't exist. (He was happy with his present equipment.)

I know others who have made a conscious decision to avoid spending. I had one friend in Montreal who said it was easier for him to save if he was not near the stores. He found a walk in the park much more enjoyable, and much less costly, than a walk through a mall. Another friend avoided reading newspapers and watching TV. He saw these media instruments as platforms for advertisers to stimulate a need in him. He felt that if he didn't see the ads, he wouldn't be tempted to spend.

Some people seem naturally frugal. I recall a neighbor from my childhood in rural Manitoba. This man would paint his farm truck once every 10 years, whether it needed it or not! We would try to calculate the vehicle's age by remembering how many times it had changed color. Yes, he may have been a tad too thrifty, but he certainly could teach us a lot about not wasting too much money on our vehicles. Another person I remember is Mr. Kubas, my grade five schoolteacher. He had one pink eraser, which at that time had already lasted him for five years! He tried to develop the same 'careful not to waste' habits in his students.

Of course, there are people on the other side of the spectrum. One person I know, with a negative net-worth (i.e. more debts than assets), traded in her one-year-old car for the latest model. When questioned why she did that, she explained that she liked the look of the dash on the new car slightly better. I then asked, "How much extra did this cost you? " She had no idea.

A lot of the money we earn goes toward paying for the need to have a car. There are two types of costs involved in having a car - ownership costs and operating costs:

1. Ownership costs include things such as depreciation (the difference between what you paid for the car and its selling price), interest, insurance, car registration and licence plate. These costs tend to be fixed and do not change with the amount that you drive. They are also incurred as soon as you decide to buy the vehicle. Using a 1998 Chevrolet Cavalier as an example, ownership costs amount to $5,741 annually.[10] These costs increase rapidly as you choose to own a more expensive vehicle.

2. Operating costs include items such as gas, oil, maintenance, etc. These costs are variable, as they are affected by how much you drive, and how well you take care of your car. A 1998 Chevrolet Cavalier costs 9.6 cents per kilometer to operate.[11] So, if the owner drove 24,000 kilometers during the year, the annual operating expenses would be $2,304.

Thus, the total annual cost of owning this car, and driving it 24,000 kilometers, is $8,045 ($5,741 + $2,304).

The following graph shows a comparative annual cost for the Chevrolet Cavalier, depending on how much you drive it. Notice that ownership costs (the large box at the bottom of the chart) account for a major portion of the total annual cost; these costs are the same, no matter if you leave the car parked in the garage, or drive it 50,000 kilometers. You cannot decrease these costs once the decision is made to own the car. All you can control are the operating costs, which are a much less significant part of the total annual cost.

[10 & 11] Canadian Automobile Association, 1998 Driving Cost.

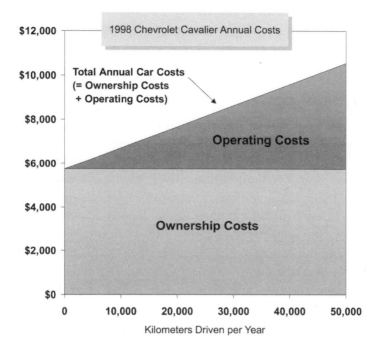

Ask yourself if it is worth $8,000 after tax, which may equate to your needing to earn about $16,000 in extra salary, just to support your need to drive this car 24,000 kilometers. Can you buy a used car so your ownership costs are greatly reduced (i.e. cut the size of the bottom box in half)? Can you trade your car in less frequently, again to reduce ownership cost? If you have two vehicles, are you able to make do with one?

Dr. J.C. Taylor, who was my finance professor at the University of Western Ontario in London, really reduced his ownership cost. He got rid of his car altogether! He calculated that he could take a taxi anywhere he wanted to go, including trips to neighboring cities, and still be money ahead.

I am emphasizing vehicle cost, because it is my experience that many people overspend in this area. Please remember that by saving only $6.50 per day, you will amass $63,750 over a 10-year period. (See the graph in the section "Your Plan" in Chapter 3, "The Basics".)

All our material needs translate into a huge need, the need for a job that provides us with money. A very wealthy person shared with me his philosophy on this subject. He feels that the need people have for a job is so strong, that it is like having an addiction. They are 'addicted' (very dependent), because they live from one paycheque to the next. If they lose the job, they are in deep financial trouble. He feels passionately that instead, they should develop an independent source of income. He feels that everyone is capable of doing this.

There are two approaches that I feel offer the best prospects for this independent source of income. The first is to use your savings to buy shares of publicly traded companies (i.e. companies listed on a stock exchange). In this way, instead of you working for the company, the company works for you. The other way is to start your own business. A primary objective should be to grow the company and hire employees, so that they can generate income for you even if you are absent. If the business is small and depends on your being there, it is really just the same as having a job.

The ultimate goal is to have sufficient money so that all your needs are met. The best way to accomplish this is to limit your material needs, and wisely invest the savings. The money earned from this investment will eventually free you from the need for a job. At this stage, you will have reached financial independence.

Chapter 6

Investment Options

Now that you have a little money set aside as a result of saving before spending, what are your options for investing it? In other words, where do you plant your seedlings so that  they will grow quickly into big healthy trees. I will discuss the options: cash investments, bonds, whole life insurance, equity, currency positions, real estate, and commodities.

I have also included a section on gambling at the end of this chapter. This would not normally be regarded as an investment option. However, the spending in this area is so great, that it is clear that many people use it as a method to try to reach financial independence.

Cash Investments

I consider cash investments to be anything that produces interest income. The essence of a cash investment is that interest is paid to you for the use of your money. This is the same concept as renting your building to someone. Rent is paid to you for the temporary use of your building, but the property remains yours, and reverts back to you at an agreed-upon date. Many Canadians have invested their savings in cash investments. My definition of these includes bank accounts, Canada Savings Bonds (a special type of bond), treasury bills, term deposits, preferred shares, guaranteed investment certificates (GICs), mortgage funds and money market funds.

As I have said, with a cash investment, you will be paid interest for the use of your money. At the end of the agreed-upon term, the principal will also be returned. However, this investment will not pay any more interest than the amount agreed upon at the outset, no matter how much was made by those who used your money. There is also no chance for a capital gain (i.e. your principal does not grow). In our tree analogy, it is like owning a mature apple tree. Each year you can harvest the apples (interest), but the tree itself (the principal) never grows. Bonds are an exception to this rule. (They are discussed later.)

The liquidity (i.e. how quickly you can convert the investment to money) varies by investment type. For example, a bank account is very liquid, because money can be taken out at any time. Canada Savings Bonds can also be cashed at any time after a brief waiting period. By contrast, term deposits lock in your money until the end of the agreed-upon term. The usual terms are one, two, three, four, and five years.

Interest income earned from cash investments is taxed at the same rate as any other income. Also, it is taxed when it is earned, not when you physically get the money. For example, you must pay taxes yearly on interest earned, even if you will only receive this money from interest five years hence.

Usually, we like our investments to be as liquid as possible, so that we can have access to them at a moment's notice. Therefore, money in a bank account, on which we may write a cheque at any time, is perceived to be better than money locked away for five years. However, there usually is a reward for investing money for a fixed term. As a general rule, the longer the term, the higher the rate of interest earned on that investment.

Financial planners advise you to try to get the best long-term rate and still remain liquid. Let's look at an example of how this is done. Suppose we wanted to invest $10,000 in a term deposit. Rather than investing the full amount for five years, we could invest $2,000 in each of 1, 2, 3, 4 and 5 year terms. As each term ends, we would reinvest the original $2,000 investment, as well as the interest earned, for a new 5-year term. Consequently, within five years, everything will be invested at 5-year rates, and one-fifth of the total investment will come due each year. Therefore, by using a bit of imagination, we can have liquidity while obtaining the 5-year rate of return.

Lastly, make sure you invest in cash-type investments only at institutions that are covered by the Canadian Deposit Insurance Corporation (CDIC), which protects up to $60,000 of your principal. All chartered Canadian banks and most trust companies carry this insurance. If they do not (and this can be confirmed by contacting CDIC at 1-800-461-2342), there is a risk that you could lose your entire investment.

Bonds

A bond is an interest-bearing certificate issued by a government or business, promising to pay the holder a specified sum on a specified date. It is a common means of raising capital. Bonds are issued for long terms e.g. 10, 20 or even 30 years. The amount of the bond, known as its face value, is usually in units of $1,000. The interest rate (usually paid twice per year) is called its coupon rate. Bonds have a definite maturity date i.e. when the bond stops paying interest and it can be cashed in. Bonds are different from other interest-bearing certificates, in that they can be bought and sold in the bond market. Therefore, bonds are very liquid because they are readily exchangeable for cash. (A

Canada Savings Bond is a special type of bond that is not traded.) Please note that when I refer to 'cash investments', I am including bonds in this definition.

Because a bond's interest rate is fixed, its market price varies with the fluctuation of interest rates in general. For example, let's assume that I knew interest rates were going to fall, but the rest of the market still had not realized this. I decide to buy a $10,000 bond that pays 10% interest and matures in 20 years. A few days later, interest rates fall to 8%. The general expectation is that interest rates will fall even further. As a result, somebody will be willing to pay me much more than $10,000 for my bond, which is locked in at a better rate than is now available. Let's say I sell this bond for $12,500, and make a $2,500 gain.

The person who bought this bond will still receive the annual interest of $1,000 (10% of $10,000). He was willing to pay up to $12,500 for the bond, because the best interest he can now receive is only 8% (8% of $12,500 also equals $1,000). In other words, the market price of the bond reflects what the bond is really worth.

In contrast, if just after I bought the bond, interest rates went up to 12% and everyone thought they would go a lot higher, no one in his right mind would pay me $10,000 for this bond. The offer price would be much lower than that, because the bond interest rate would now be below the current rate. If I sold this bond, I would lose money.

There are two ways to make money from bonds. The first way is to earn the interest that they pay. All you have to do is hold the bond, and it earns interest as long as it is held. This is identical to owning a GIC. The other way is that you can speculate that interest rates will go up or down, and buy or sell accordingly. If large amounts are involved, fortunes can be made or lost very quickly.

Assuming that a 10-year GIC has the same interest rate as a 10-year bond, there really is no difference in the value of what you buy (both lock your money in at that rate for 10 years). The only difference is that the bond can be resold in the bond market at its current market value. A GIC has no market value. Some people feel worried when the bond market value fluctuates, and feel safer with the GIC. However, in my opinion, the risk is the same.

Whole Life Insurance

This investment instrument mixes the purchasing of an investment with the buying of life insurance. The investment part of the package is usually linked to a stock exchange index (a term that will be explained later), or a term deposit. The insurance company charges a fee for putting together this package – this is how they make their money. Some brand names for whole life insurance are Freedom Fifty-Five and Universal Life.

The monthly premiums (what you pay each month) will stop after a number of years e.g. twenty-five. The reason for this is that the invested portion is now either earning enough interest to pay for the annual insurance cost, or it equals the death benefit.

Many policies allow the policy owner to borrow up to 75% of the invested portion. This may not be as attractive as it appears. If you had invested the money in your own savings account, you could 'borrow' 100%!

I avoid whole life insurance, as I believe that a better rate of return can be made using other investments. I prefer to buy insurance separately, instead of linking it to investing.

Equity

Equity refers to owning the shares of corporations. It also includes mutual funds and participation units.

Almost all big business is conducted through corporations e.g. Royal Bank, Wal-Mart, and McDonald's. They are owned by their shareholders, who each hold some common shares (equity). Share ownership effectively gives the holder the right to a portion of the company's earnings. By selling these shares, the corporation raises money that is used to help finance business operations.

If the corporation does well, i.e. has growing sales and profits, the value of the share also grows. People are always anxious to own a good thing, and are therefore willing to pay more and more for each share. Alternatively, if the company does poorly, the share value won't go up and may even go down.

The key point to remember is that the shareholders own the corporation. Corporations that are publicly traded, which means their shares are bought and sold on a stock exchange, often have millions of shares outstanding. Most individual investors own only a very small part of a corporation. This brings out another very important point. Equity investments in most large corporations are usually very liquid. Many large corporations, such as Intel and Coke, have millions of shares traded each day. With so many shares changing hands, it is easy to exchange some or all of your shares for someone else's cash.

Trading centers, where people gather to exchange shares, are called stock exchanges. The American, NASDAQ (National Association of Security Dealers Automated Quotation) and New York Stock Exchanges are all based in New York City. In Canada, there are the Toronto, Montreal, Vancouver, and Alberta Stock Exchanges. There is also a Canadian Unlisted Exchange (often called Over The

Counter), which is our equivalent to the NASDAQ. Note that company stocks are usually traded on one or two exchanges, but not on all of them. There are exchanges in almost every major country in the world. Examples include London, Hong Kong and Nikkei (which is in Tokyo).

Over the years, I have worked on the financial matters of hundreds of individuals. I believe that the single biggest error I have seen is the lack of equity in investment portfolios. The second biggest error is the wrong choice of equity. Both these matters will be discussed in more depth later.

All of my investments, apart from real estate, are in equity. This is a deliberate strategy.

Currency Positions

Most countries have their own currency. Its value, relative to other currencies, fluctuates. For example, during the 1980's, the value of the Japanese yen rose relative to the Canadian and U.S. dollars.

The Canadian dollar used to be worth more than the U.S. dollar. At the time of this writing, it has dropped to 69% of the U.S. currency. Therefore, a Canadian dollar cannot buy as much in world goods as can an American dollar. Canadians lost 'world purchasing power'. It is much more expensive for a Canadian to spend a few months in Florida now, than it would have been before.

Russians have lost 90% of their wealth relative to the American dollar over the last five years! The people of Indonesia have lost 84% of their wealth in less than a year! We can protect ourselves from currency devaluation by purchasing investments in a currency that we believe is strong. For example, the Indonesian citizen who had the equivalent of $500,000 U.S. dollars of purchasing power a short while ago has now only $80,000 (16% of $500,000). What a hit to take in less than a year!

Currency fluctuations open up the opportunity for astute investors to make a lot of money, by taking advantage of a change in currency exchange rates that they can foresee coming. If you know a currency is under or over valued, you can buy or sell this currency in the futures market and make a handsome profit. However, I do not believe the average investor should speculate on currency changes.

There is one very important point I want to get across. Our assets, e.g. real estate, term deposits, or shares, are always valued in some currency. The relative value of this currency has a silent but very real impact on our wealth, even though we may not be aware of it. Our true wealth (purchasing power) is dependent upon the value of the asset, as well as the value of the currency in which it is held. No serious investor can afford to ignore this.

Real Estate

Another investment option is real estate. Many people, however, do not own real estate and rent their accommodations instead. For others, their home and/or cottage is their only real estate investment. Some may invest in this area by owning rental property.

There was a time when real estate did very well nationwide. This was when many baby boomers were leaving home and starting their own families. Generally, the 'glow' on real estate investment has dimmed in recent years. However, in selected areas it continues to be a lucrative investment.

The main problem with real estate is that it is usually a very large investment, and it is not very liquid. Unlike a bank account, where we can write a cheque and take out part of the investment, we have to sell an entire real estate investment to get our hands on any cash. It is also possible that when you need to sell your house or commercial property, you may have difficulty finding a buyer.

Another consideration, and one that people don't often think of, is that real estate is usually held in local dollars. If you need U.S. dollars because you want to spend winters in Florida, and your only income is from Canadian real estate rentals, you may fall short if the Canadian currency falls relative to the U.S. currency. Cash investments and equities allow you to buy assets in a foreign currency. This way, you can have the required savings in U.S. dollars, and you will not have to worry about currency fluctuations.

Another way around this is to buy real estate in the U.S. itself. However, this usually brings with it all sorts of complications, such as absentee management, foreign taxes and foreign laws. These are problems that even I, as an accountant, would not dream of touching.

Owning a rental property is not always an easy way to make money. First of all, as a landlord, you may have a tenant who does not pay the rent. Do you really want the aggravation of evicting someone? I don't. Also, having done the tax returns of many landlords, I am always amazed at the amount spent on repairs and maintenance. I believe that these costs are usually underestimated when the rental unit is purchased.

There are two keys to making a good investment in real estate. The first is to buy a property in the right location, and the second is to buy it at the right price. When purchasing, it is important to bear in mind whether the value of real estate in the local area is appreciating or depreciating, and if this trend is likely to continue. Also, before you buy the property, ask yourself if it could be resold quickly, if you needed the cash.

It is obvious that a real estate investment is not my first love. I own my own office (a commercial condominium) and my house. I have no intention of investing in any other real estate. I believe that problems inherent in real estate investments outweigh their potential gain, especially when compared to other options. I have reviewed many people's investments in this area, and I am not impressed. I know very few people who have made really good returns from their investments in real estate.

However, I do recommend that you own the roof over your head. There is a very important reason for this. It is an example of saving before spending. If you own your own dwelling, then at some point you will no longer be committed to mortgage or rental payments. By that time, you will have accumulated an asset of substantial value. As well, you can live much more inexpensively if you aren't making mortgage or rental payments. So, even if your house or condo does not offer the best return on investment, it is still very valuable as a forced savings plan. There is also the bonus of pride in ownership.

Commodities

The commodity markets provide a fascinating investment opportunity. In this market, people trade the rights (ownership) to commodities, which are basic items or staple goods that are bought and sold. Examples include grain, oil, gold, silver, cattle, soybeans, etc. Many fortunes have been made and lost in the commodity market. One famous example was the rush on tulip bulbs in Holland in the 1630's. These bulbs were imported from Constantinople by the flower loving Dutch. Demand outstripped supply, and even middle class and poor people began buying them purely as an investment. The price of tulip bulbs kept going up. A single bulb could fetch the price of 12 sheep or 1000 pounds of cheese! Suddenly in 1637, the Dutch realized the absurdity of these prices. The value of the bulbs plunged overnight, wiping out the wealth of many individuals. In fact, so many people were involved in this market disaster that it temporarily crushed Holland's economy.

Another more recent example was the attempt by the Hunt family of Texas to corner the silver market in 1979. They tried to buy up the world's supply of silver at low prices. Their plan was to let only limited quantities onto the market at very high prices, and thereby make a fortune. But they ran short of money before the plan could be completed, and lost a bundle instead.

I have very few clients who invest in this area. However, farmers (like my relatives in Manitoba) do use commodity markets to lock in the price they will receive for their produce, be it grain, honey or something else. This is how it works. The farmers feel that the price for their product is definitely going to change, for example, decrease. They decide in the spring to sell a certain amount of product at a given price for delivery in the fall (this is called futures). Therefore, they know now what they will get for their crop, because they have locked in the price. If their hunch is wrong i.e. the price increases, they will lose money, because they have to sell their crop at the agreed upon price, which is lower than the going rate. This process can also take place if they do not have product to sell. However, when the future comes due, they will have to buy the product at the current price, in order to have it available to deliver.

The commodities market is a very specialized field, and is not an area in which the average person should invest. However, certain people, providing they have in depth knowledge of a specific commodity, can do well. One individual I knew ran a manufacturing company that used a great quantity of a particular type of metal. After many years, he became very expert at monitoring the key variables that affected its future price. He would advise his company to buy the rights to this commodity when prices were low. Therefore, their product costs were less than that of their competitors, and the company was very successful. It is my belief that it takes this type of insight, along with great discipline and nerves of steel, to make money from commodities.

Gambling

The Canadian gambling industry is huge. No one is certain of its exact size. The United Church estimates annual spending to be between $20 to $27 billion![12] Statistics Canada calculates its size to be 10% larger than the Canadian logging and forestry industry![13]

Let's examine one popular form of gambling known as "Nevada Tickets". They are sold at bingo halls, service stations and many other retail outlets. Each ticket costs 50 cents, and prizes range from 50 cents to $100. The tickets come in boxes of 2,184 each. The box pays out prize money of exactly $800, but sells for $1,092 (2184 tickets @ 50 cents each). Therefore, for every box sold, the purchasers as a group lose $292 ($1,092-$800), or 27% of what they paid ($292 ÷ $1092)! In other words, for every $1 you spend, you will lose 27 cents.

---

[12] United Church of Canada Web Site: "Gambling in Canada – A Multi-Billion-Dollar Industry".

[13] Statistics Canada "Prospective on Labour and Income Catalog #75-01-XPE".

Assume you spend $3,377 per year on gambling. Remember that's after-tax income. The casino's payoff is typically 56%. Your resulting annual loss would be $1,485 (44% of $3,377). There are associated costs such as food, drink, transportation and accommodations when you go to a casino. I assumed this related cost to be $915 annually. Therefore, you lose $2,400 ($1,485 + $915) per year on gambling. Assuming you are taxed at the 40% tax rate, you have to earn about $4,000 per year to cover the $2,400 loss. Remember that the same $2,400, if invested in an RRSP, would be worth $63,750 after 10 years!

The reason gambling is so popular is that people are 'probability blind'. This concept (where people cannot correctly assess the odds) is discussed in detail in Chapter 8, "Risk".

Going to bingo, betting on horse races, etc. can be a form of recreation. My mother loves playing bingo (and guts poker, which she claims she is good at) with her friends every Sunday night. However, she sets a spending limit for herself before she goes. If you are going to gamble for entertainment, I advise you to do the same.

The amount of money spent on gambling provides me with great hope. It demonstrates that there is no shortage of money, just a shortage of knowledge. If this problem can be rectified, the financial well being of many will be greatly improved.

Why not take the 'other-hand' approach? Every time you open your wallet to spend a dollar on a lottery ticket, use your other hand to immediately put another dollar into your pocket. Use this money to buy RRSPs. See which method of investing actually wins! By saving $6.50 a day, and investing it at 18%, you will have $16,000,000 in 40 years! See Appendix for details.

What to Do

There are many investment options. Equity, cash investments, and real estate are the most viable for the average person. Of these, I much prefer equity.

When you choose the cash investment option e.g. a term deposit, you are receiving interest by lending money to the bank. The bank turns around and lends this money to someone else, often a company, at a higher rate of interest than you are receiving. The bank keeps the profit, which is made from the resulting spread in the interest rates. Meanwhile, the company that has borrowed the money from the bank makes improvements in its operations e.g. new plant or equipment. It starts to show more of a profit, and pays back the loan plus interest to the bank. So, both the bank and the company that borrowed your money make a profit from using it. Why lend your money to banks and businesses, when it is just as easy to be an owner of these same corporations by purchasing their stocks? You will earn a better return.

Andex Associates Inc. compared the results of four different investment options. In each case, $100 Canadian was invested for 48 years (1950 - 1997). The table below summarizes the findings without considering inflation. (The average inflation rate for this period was 4.3%. To have the same purchasing power as $100 in 1950 dollars, you would need $739 in 1997 dollars).

Investment Comparisons		
$100 Invested in 1950	**Avg. rate of return**	**Value in 1997**
US Stocks	13.4%	$39,477
Cdn. Stocks	11.4%	$14,684
Cdn. 5-year GICs	7.9%	$ 3,696
Cdn. 90-day Treasury Bills	6.5%	$ 1,952

The information in the chart drives home a couple of points:

1. It was much more profitable to invest in stocks rather than cash investments i.e. GICs and treasury bills.
2. It paid to choose long-term rather than short-term cash investments. In the end, the long-term GIC was worth 89% more than the short-term treasury bill.
3. It paid to invest in U.S. stocks rather than Canadian stocks. The 2% difference between their rates of return had an enormous impact on their end value ($39,477 versus $14,684)!
4. An investment in U.S. stocks was worth 20 times the investment in treasury bills ($39,477 versus $1,952)!

It is important to note that the chart does not address the impact of taxes. Income from stocks is taxed at a much lower rate than income from cash investments. (This subject will be discussed in detail in Chapter 9, "Income Taxes".) This tax advantage, coupled with their superior rate of return, makes stocks the obvious investment choice. I therefore urge you to seriously consider stocks as an investment option.

That being said, you must also consider how comfortable you are with investment volatility. If the value of your portfolio declines, and you have trouble sleeping at night, you should only be in cash investments. If, on the other hand, you can watch your investments dramatically drop in value and not bat an eye, you have the stamina required to own shares. If you have a medium tolerance to volatility, choose participation units fully explained in the next chapter.

The following graph illustrates the recommended investment options depending on your personality.

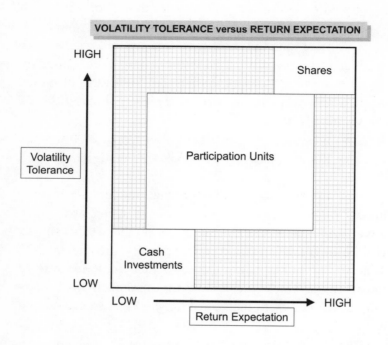

Chapter 7

Equity – Diving Deeper

Let's assume that you would like to buy equity. For example, you may want to buy shares in a specific company. (Investors usually buy shares in several different companies to diversify their holdings.) How do you actually do it? There are several options available.

Where to Buy Equity

One way is to use a full-service broker e.g. RBC Securities, Nesbitt Burns, Wood Gundy, Merrill Lynch, ScotiaMcleod, etc. They will discuss your investment needs, and help you decide which shares to buy. You must deposit money at an account opened at the brokerage firm. This is almost identical to a regular bank account. An investment order will be issued to purchase these shares on your behalf. The money for the cost of the shares, and the commission for the broker, will be withdrawn from your account. A few days later, you will receive written confirmation of your purchase.

Another way is to use a discount broker. The most commonly known example is the TD Green Line, but every major bank owns one e.g. CT Securities, InvestorLine, Investors Edge, Action Direct, etc. Discount brokers charge less to buy or sell shares than the full-service firms, but they provide no investment advice. You open an account with them by filling out a form at your local bank. All transactions are handled via a 1-800-telephone number connecting you to their office, located in a large centre such as Montreal or Toronto. You may also use the Internet to place orders with a discount broker.

Lastly, you could contact a financial planner. They cannot buy or sell company shares as a broker can, unless they are licensed to do so (most are not). Financial planners generally sell mutual funds.

Now that we have covered where to buy equity, we can review types of equity available, namely mutual funds, participation units and company shares.

Mutual Funds

A mutual fund is the name given to a special trust, in which people pool their money for investment purposes. This pool of funds, which all the investors share, is used to buy shares, bonds, treasury bills, mortgages, and related investments. Generally, equity mutual funds own many shares, and tend to perform much like the overall stock market. Investors can buy into the fund or redeem their money at any time, but there may be some penalties.

Some equity mutual funds specialize in certain types of companies, countries or investment strategies. For example, a mutual fund may concentrate in such areas as utilities, blue chip, hi-tech, gold, growth, or mining companies. Some may buy companies operating just in Asia, Europe, Latin America or the U.S.A. The fund may include different combinations of the above.

A mutual fund corporation (a corporation that manages a mutual fund and owns the fund's name e.g. Templeton) is very separate from the invested funds (which are collectively owned by the investors). The corporation makes money by paying itself an annual fee (commonly over 2% of the fund's stock market value). Most people are not aware of this fee, as it is not billed directly to them. Instead, this payment is removed from the investors' pool of money.

You may say that an annual fee of 2% does not sound like much. However, let me show you another way of looking at it. For example, assume that one of the interest investments that your mutual fund holds is a Canada Savings Bond, which pays 5% annually. Since you are charged 2% of the value of the bond to have it managed, this leaves you with a return of only 3%. Why not buy the investment directly and double your return?

In the summary section of Chapter 6, "Investment Options", we looked at investment results over the past 48 years, and saw how significant a 2% difference in return was ($100 grew to $39,447 instead of $14,684). Annual fees do matter. With a 2% annual fee, you will lose 50% of your investment over 25 years. I'll show you how to outperform most mutual funds without paying these fees.

Besides the annual fee, there is usually a sales fee that you must pay. If it is paid at the time you buy the fund, this sales fee is known as a front-end load. It is commonly 3%, and is deducted from the money you want invested. A much more common selling fee is the back-end load. This fee (usually 6%) is largely hidden, because the investor only pays it when he sells the fund. The longer you hold the fund, the less the back end load will be. (It usually declines by $3/4$% for each full year you hold the fund.) Some mutual funds even advertise that they have no loads. Don't forget, though, that no matter what the loads are, the mutual fund corporation is always collecting an annual fee.

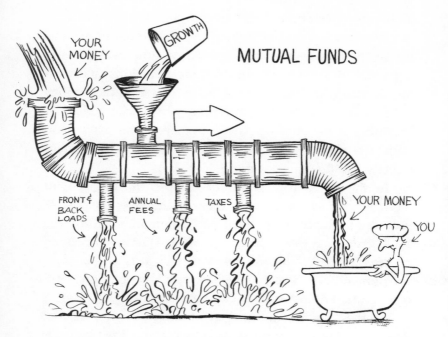

Mutual fund corporations strive to sell more funds, so that they can earn more fees. To accomplish this goal of increased sales, they utilize three distinct marketing methods - independent sales agents, captive sales force, and self-marketing:

1. The 'independent agent' marketing method uses agents such as financial planners and stockbrokers to sell their product. Examples of companies using this very popular marketing method include Trimark, Templeton and BPI. Each mutual fund corporation must reward the agent well, so that he will promote its fund. The selling organization, e.g. RBC Securities, shares the 3% front end load or 6% back end load with the financial advisor. They both also share an annual fee of between $1/2\%$ and 1% of the fund's value, as long as the investor stays with that fund.

2. The 'captive sales force' is when the mutual fund corporation has its own sales force, which sells only its funds. Investors Group is by far the largest corporation using this approach. It generally charges a front end load for investments under $10,000, and a back end load on all investments. Banks also use this marketing method, but some will also sell you funds other than their own. Banks usually do not charge front or back end loads.

3. The 'self-marketing' approach is where the mutual fund company tries to attract customers directly. No sales agents are used. The best example of this approach is Altamira, which advertises and markets its own funds. There usually are no front or back end fees on these types of mutual funds. The company makes its money from the annual fees, paid to itself from the pool of funds the investors trusted it to manage.

Let me emphasize that you should be aware of how sales agents are paid. (We frequently seek their financial advice.) Obviously, people working for commissions will not promote the sale of products for which they receive no payback.

Here is an analogy. If you did not know which new car to buy, you may start out by visiting your neighborhood Toyota dealership. The salesperson would recommend a Tercel, Corolla, or Camry, depending on your needs and what you could afford. He would never mention the options available at other dealerships or on the Internet! Perhaps a better starting point in this decision making process would be to read a consumer magazine, which reviews all new cars and ranks them by quality and cost.

Now, let's assume your RRSP has $100,000 in GICs, and you decide you want a better return. You visit an independent financial planner or broker. If he sells you a back end equity mutual fund, he will immediately share the $6,000 load fee with the organization that employs him. He would not recommend that you buy funds from Altamira, Investors Group, or a bank, because doing that would not pay him.

Participation Units

Please pay careful attention to this section, as I believe participation units should play a pivotal role in your portfolio.

To really understand participation units, you must first understand the stock market term 'index'. It is a specific group of shares which is constantly monitored for value. For example, the grand daddy of all indices (plural of index) is the Dow Jones Industrial Average, which was originated by Mr. Jones. He took 12 shares on the New York Stock Exchange, totaled their dollar value, and divided this number by 12 to find the average price. The resulting number was the first 'Dow Jones Industrial Average'. Therefore, the index number means nothing in itself, but it does provide investors with a means of judging market direction, when it is compared to itself at different times. For example, if the Dow Jones Industrial Average was at 7,900 points and went to 7,979 points, the New York market is said to have gone up 79 basis points or 1%.

The Toronto 35 index is an example of an index that reflects what is happening on the Toronto Stock Exchange. The following chart shows the 35 companies that make it up.

Toronto 35 Index	
1. Abitibi-Price	19. National Bank
2. Alcan Aluminum	20. Noranda Inc.
3. Bank of Montreal	21. Northern Telecom
4. Bank of Nova Scotia	22. NOVA Corporation
5. Barrick Gold	23. Petro-Canada
6. BCE Inc.	24. Placer Dome
7. Bombardier	25. Renaissance Energy
8. Canadian Imperial Bank	26. Rogers Communications
9. Canadian Oxy Petroleum	27. Royal Bank
10. Canadian Pacific Ltd.	28. Seagram Co. (The)
11. Canadian Tire	29. Talisman Energy
12. Dofasco Inc.	30. Teck Corp.
13. Imasco Ltd.	31. Thomson Corporation
14. Inco Limited	32. Toronto-Dominion Bank
15. Laidlaw Inc.	33. TransAlta Corporation
16. MacMillan Bloedel	34. TransCanada PipeLines
17. Magna Int'l	35. TVX Gold
18. Moore Corp.	

A participation unit is a basket of real shares, which is held in trust for the investor, and trades like a share on the stock exchange. It is administered by the stock exchange itself. One participation unit, called TIPS, holds the same shares as the ones used to calculate the Toronto 35 Index (listed above). 'TIPS' stands for Toronto Index Participation Units. This participation unit trades as a share (its symbol is TIP) on the Toronto Stock Exchange.

The following table shows you what it looks like when it's listed in the financial papers.

TORONTO

52-week high	low Stock	Sym	Div	High	Low	Close	Chg	Vol (100s)	Yield	P/E ratio
1.10	0.38 Tonko Dev	TAK		0.39	0.39	0.39	-0.01	5000		19.5
1.51	0.65 Torex Res	TRX		0.85	0.85	0.85	-0.05	191		
23.00	14.25 Toromont	TIH	0.26	16.75	16.50	16.50	-0.25	676	1.6	13.0
42.90	29.00 TIPS 35	TIP	0.72	35.40	34.55	34.85	-0.65	14456	2.0	
47.95	32.50 TIPS 100	HIP	0.74	39.30	38.65	38.85	-0.65	3770	1.9	
74.75	37.50 ♣ TD Bank	TD	1.36	45.50	44.40	44.45	-0.65	10657	3.1	11.6
30.75	27.50 ♣ TD B	TD.PR.H	1.78	28.70	28.60	28.60	-0.10	32	6.2	
27.05	14.00 Torstar nv	TS.B	0.58	18.35	18.25	18.25	-0.15	646	3.2	14.5

My favorite participation unit is Standard and Poors Depository Receipts (SPYDERS). It holds the same 500 shares as the ones used in the S&P 500 Index, and trades on the American Stock Exchange.

AMERICAN

52-week high	low Stock	Sym	High	Low	Close	Chg	Vol (100s)
$31\frac{1}{4}$	$7\frac{1}{8}$ 7 Seas	SEV	$9\frac{7}{16}$	$8\frac{3}{4}$	$8\frac{3}{4}$	$-\frac{9}{16}$	678
$2\frac{1}{2}$	$\frac{5}{8}$ Sheffield	SHM	$1\frac{15}{16}$	$1\frac{3}{4}$	$1\frac{3}{4}$		824
$9\frac{7}{8}$	$4\frac{7}{16}$ Sonus	SSN	$4\frac{5}{8}$	$4\frac{7}{16}$	$4\frac{9}{16}$	$-\frac{3}{16}$	45
$119\frac{15}{64}$	$90\frac{3}{32}$ S&P Dep R	SPY	$114\frac{1}{4}$	$112\frac{1}{2}$	$113\frac{5}{16}$	$-\frac{13}{16}$	61887
$73\frac{3}{4}$	$51\frac{7}{32}$ S&P Midcp	MDY	$68\frac{5}{32}$	$66\frac{53}{64}$	$67\frac{1}{4}$	$-1\frac{5}{64}$	4714
$34\frac{3}{8}$	$15\frac{1}{4}$ ♣ Stillwatr	SWC	$33\frac{3}{4}$	$32\frac{1}{4}$	$32\frac{1}{2}$	$-1\frac{3}{8}$	1911
$50\frac{1}{8}$	$30\frac{5}{8}$ Tel Data	TDS	$40\frac{5}{8}$	$39\frac{7}{8}$	$40\frac{1}{8}$	$-\frac{1}{8}$	808
$9\frac{1}{2}$	$2\frac{7}{16}$ ♣ Texas Biot	TXB	$5\frac{1}{4}$	$4\frac{9}{16}$	$4\frac{13}{16}$	$-\frac{5}{16}$	2049

My second favorite participation unit is DIAMONDS, which reflects The Dow Jones Industrial Average. There are also participation units to reflect specific countries. These are called WEBS (World Equity Benchmark Shares).

The following chart lists commonly known participation units, the index each reflects, and the stock market on which it can be found. TSE stands for the Toronto Stock Exchange. AMEX stands for American Stock Exchange.

PARTICIPATION UNITS			
BASED ON	ACRONYM	STOCK SYMBOL	EXCHANGE
TSE 35	TIPS	TIP	TSE
TSE 100	HIPS	HIP	TSE
Dow Jones Industrial Avg.	DIAMONDS	DIA	AMEX
S&P 500	SPYDERS	SPY	AMEX
Australia Market	Australia WEBS	EWA	AMEX
Austria Market	Austria WEBS	EWO	AMEX
Belgium Market	Belgium WEBS	EWK	AMEX
Canada Market	Canada WEBS	EWC	AMEX
France Market	France WEBS	EWQ	AMEX
Germany Market	Germany WEBS	EWG	AMEX
Hong Kong Market	Hong Kong WEBS	EWH	AMEX
Italy Market	Italy WEBS	EWI	AMEX
Japan Market	Japan WEBS	EWJ	AMEX
Malaysia Market	Malaysia WEBS	EWM	AMEX
Mexico Market	Mexico WEBS	EWW	AMEX
Netherlands Market	Netherlands WEBS	EWN	AMEX
Singapore Market	Singapore WEBS	EWS	AMEX
Spain Market	Spain WEBS	EWP	AMEX
Sweden Market	Sweden WEBS	EWD	AMEX
Switzerland Market	Switzerland WEBS	EWL	AMEX
United Kingdom Market	United Kingdom WEBS	EWU	AMEX

Let's examine why participation units are one of the stock markets' best kept secrets.

Simplicity: Buying participation units is an easy way to buy a diversified investment portfolio. (By buying TIPS you are buying into 35 different companies, and that is more than enough diversity.) It fits into my thinking of keeping things simple, as participation units are much less complex than mutual funds. You always know what shares you hold, as they are not constantly changing as they are in a mutual fund.

By purchasing TIPS, you have only one investment. By hearing the stock market reports (index numbers), you instantly know how you are doing, because TIPS exactly mirrors the TSE 35. By contrast, many people have a plethora of mutual funds. Their affairs are so complex that they have no idea of what they really own, or how they are doing.

Liquidity: Is it easy to sell participation units and obtain cash, if you need some money? Yes. TIPS and HIPS are two of the most marketable equities in Canada. DIAMONDS and SPYDERS are two of the most marketable equities in the world.

Fees: The annual fee for TIPS is .05% of the value of units held. This is a negligible amount compared to the 2% fee charged by some mutual funds. The 2% annual mutual fund fee is 40 times the annual participation unit fee!

The only sales fee you must pay is the cost to buy or sell the participation unit. This cost is the same as buying or selling any other share. Remember that mutual funds, on the other hand, usually charge a back-end load fee of 6%. If you bought and then sold a back-end fee mutual fund, you would usually lose 6% of your investment!

Dividends: With participation units, all dividends received from the companies held in the portfolio flow through to the unit holder. This flow through may not be true for all mutual funds. Sometimes the fund keeps the dividends as an indirect fee.

Taxes: Participation units attract less tax than do mutual funds. The mutual fund managers constantly buy and sell shares, as they try to outperform the market. The gains made by the fund are passed on to you as taxable capital gains (less any losses) in the year that they occur. The fund itself pays no taxes. You, the holder, pay them. On the other hand, participation units do not trade the shares that they hold. Therefore, there are almost no taxable capital gains generated, until you sell the participation unit itself.

As a mutual fund holder, you must track these capital gains and losses that you have already paid tax on, to know your correct tax cost base. This can be a complicated process, but if you do not do this, you may be paying taxes twice on some capital gains.

Be aware of hidden tax problems with mutual funds. When you buy the fund, it could own company shares that have significantly appreciated in value. When these shares are sold, the market value of the fund has not been affected. The fund simply has cash instead of shares. (The market value of the fund is always determined by the stock market value of all the shares, as well as the cash that it holds.) But, all of the capital gain, accumulated from the date the stock was first purchased, is assigned to the people who happen to hold the mutual fund at the time of the stock sale. It is possible for an individual to buy a mutual fund, experience no increase in fund value, but nevertheless be responsible for taxes of the large capital gain.

RRSPs: Like mutual funds, participation units can be held as Canadian or foreign content within RRSP investments. TIPS and HIPS qualify as Canadian content. DIAMONDS and WEBS are also eligible RRSP investments, but count as foreign content. Please note that Revenue Canada has recently ruled that SPYDERS is not an eligible RRSP investment. In future, there is a chance that DIAMONDS and WEBS will also not be eligible.

<u>Performance</u>: The best reason for owning participation units is their performance. From 1991 to 1997, TIPS doubled in value (even taking into account its first year of negative growth of minus 7%). For the same time period, SPYDERS tripled in value. During the past 15 years, SPYDERS has had just two years of negative growth (minus 1% and minus 3%). The annual growth over the past three years has been impressive at 39%, 23% and 34%. The following graph shows the annual rates of return for the S&P 500 index for the last 10 years.

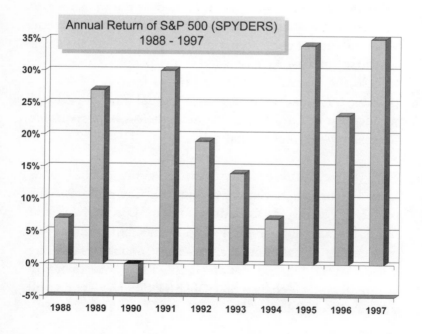

The cumulative effect can be dramatic. The next graph shows the results if you invested $1,000 in SPYDERS on January 1, 1988.

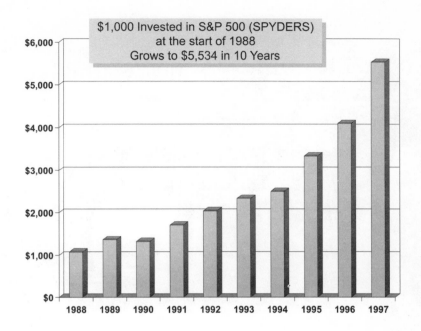

On a comparative basis, the following statistic speaks for itself:

During the past 10 years, participation units outperformed 93% of equity mutual funds![14]

---

[14] The Finanical Post (June 13-15, 1998) reported that over a 10-year period, SPYDERS outperformed 93% of all U.S. equity mutual funds. There is every reason to believe that the same was true for participation units in Canada.

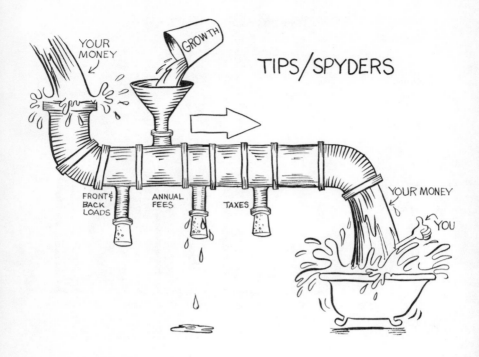

Company Shares

I prefer to hold shares directly, instead of through an intermediary such as a mutual fund.

The attractive features about owning shares, rather than cash investments, are that shares have better liquidity, long-term growth, and flexibility. If you want to cash in your shares, simply direct your broker to sell. You will have your cash within three days. Shares are considered a good long-term investment, because you own part of the company's future growth. Furthermore, equity offers the luxury of flexibility. You can sell any portion of your investment, or all of it, at any time you choose.

I never buy a share unless it is listed on one of the major exchanges, e.g. Toronto, New York, or NASDAQ Stock Exchange. Their listings include big solid companies with names you would recognize e.g. Coca-Cola, Bombardier, Seagram, Wrigley, Hershey, Quaker Oats and Merck.

Stock exchanges operate independently from each other. In order to be listed on an exchange, a company must pay a fee. Some companies may wish to list their shares on several exchanges. The price of a stock may vary slightly from one exchange to another. If prices are different, investors buy some shares on the exchange where the price is lower, and sell the same number of shares on the exchange where the price is higher. A profit is made without a risk being taken, because they still own what they did before. This practice is called 'arbitrage'. It keeps shares trading at about the same price on the various exchanges on which they are listed.

Arbitrage can help protect your investment. For example, Seagram is traded on several exchanges i.e. New York, Montreal, and Toronto. The New York Stock Exchange is by far the largest of these exchanges, and it therefore determines Seagram's share price. If the value of the Canadian dollar dropped a lot, the share price on the Toronto and Montreal exchanges would increase (due to arbitrage) to match the Canadian equivalent on the New York Stock Exchange. You, as the Canadian investor owning Seagram shares, would not lose the value of your money. Note that Canadian term deposits, even if government guaranteed, would not offer you the same amount of protection.

I have compiled a chart of price comparisons of high-quality stocks, to illustrate the rates of return available. The chart compares the mean price (an average price excluding extremes) of particular stocks in 1982, to the stock price recorded as of October 1996. With this information, it is not difficult to determine the growth of a particular investment during this time period. All prices are stated in U.S. dollars.

PRICE COMPARISON OF QUALITY STOCKS

NAME	1982 Price (mean)	1996 Price (October)	% Change
Abbott Laboratories	2	50	2,400
Anheuser Busch	9	39	333
Block (H&R)	4	28	600
Bristol- Myers-Squibb	16	97	506
Coca Cola	1.5	51	3,300
Dun & Bradstreet	20	61	205
General Electric	19	95	400
General Mills	8	59	637
Gillette Co.	5	73	1,360
Heinz (H.J.)	2.7	34	1,159
Hewlett-Packard	15	45	200
Johnson & Johnson	10	52	420
Kellogg Co.	7	67	857
McDonald's Corp.	8	46	475
Merck & Co.	4	70	1,650
Minnesota Mining & Mfg (3M)	16	69	331
Pall Corp.	6	27	350
PepsiCo Inc.	2.5	28	1,020
Pfizer Inc.	16	79	393
Philip Morris	7	93	1,228
Procter & Gamble	13	98	653

These results are very impressive. When you combine an excellent rate of return with all of the other benefits of equity, it is hard not to be a fan of owning quality company shares.

How does one know when a stock will yield a high rate of return? Does the stock represent good value? The short answer is that no one knows for certain.

There is a term called 'book value per share' that is frequently used in the investment industry. It represents how much each share is worth if the company stopped all operations and sold its assets. This value usually provides the lower extreme to which shares may fall. This is one indication of value.

The key factor that affects the future value of the shares is how well the company is doing. If the company is very profitable, people are willing to pay a premium to be a partial owner of such a moneymaking machine. As a result, the stock price rises due to this increased demand for these shares. (A company that makes a lot of money will always have a rising book value.)

Share prices are also affected by something that is not within our control, i.e. the price other people are willing to pay for the share. Since I have no control over what other people do or think, I try to ignore this factor. If the price of a share, which I already consider to be a bargain, goes down, I'll buy more. I'm a very patient investor. If you do not borrow to invest, you can afford to be patient. Long term, a successful company will be recognized by the market.

I discuss company shares in more depth in Chapter 13, "Finding Value".

Chapter 8

Risk

"The first step to knowledge is to know that we are ignorant."
-Lord David Cecil

Risk is about calculating the probabilities of future events. However, many people appear to be 'probability blind'. Psychologists Amos  Tversky and Daniel Kahneman have gathered many examples of how people's personal beliefs (their own assessment of risk) are not statistically accurate. To illustrate:

People fear travel by plane more than by car, although plane travel is statistically much safer.

People fear nuclear power, although more people are injured or killed during the process of mining and burning coal to generate power.

People gamble at casinos and buy lottery tickets. But, since the 'house' must obviously make a profit, the players, on average, must lose.

Tversky and Kahneman have concluded that "the human mind is not designed to grasp the laws of probability, even though these laws rule the universe".[15] The media makes it more difficult to understand real probabilities by sensationalizing stories (e.g. large lottery winners and aircraft disasters). Our minds like and retain the dramatic events, instead of the everyday ones. If the average person

---

[15] "How the Mind Works", Stephen Pinker.

logically assessed risk, we would not have bingo, lottery tickets, casinos, or any other form of pubic gambling. However, since gambling is a huge industry, it is evident that we want to follow our own beliefs - not the logical laws of probability.

Just knowing that we have a 'probability blind' limitation is a giant step forward in making the correct investment decisions.

Investment Risk Defined

Many people place their trust in cash investments to avoid risk. I buy shares to avoid the same risk. With regard to the stock market, I believe that most people do not accurately assess probability. They place too much emphasis on market fluctuations, and undervalue long-term growth. All risks considered, I think it is safer to invest in quality shares than to keep your money in cash investments.

I see risk as any danger to the future purchasing power of my investments. I want to build enough wealth through investments, so that some day I can live a certain lifestyle without having to work. Risk is anything that threatens this dream. Therefore, to my way of thinking, it is risky to place all my money in cash investments (e.g. Canadian government guaranteed term deposits), because they do not increase in value as quickly as shares. Also, I am subjecting my future purchasing power (e.g. a winter trip to Florida) to the whims of Canadian currency fluctuations. I can avoid this problem by owning shares of U.S corporations, which are tied to the stronger U.S. currency.

A short time ago, a major part of our country was facing a very critical decision. Quebec citizens went to the polls to decide whether or not to remain part of our federation. The results of this referendum were uncomfortably close. There was a very real possibility that our country was about to break up.

Just before the referendum, many Canadians wanted to keep their assets 'safe', and so chose to place their investments in federal government guaranteed term deposits. Others took their cash out of the Bank of Montreal in Montreal, and placed it in the Bank of Montreal in Cornwall, Ontario. These actions did little to minimize the real risk on their Canadian dollar investments. Had the people of Quebec voted to separate, the Canadian currency everywhere would have lost a lot of value.

Other people traded their Canadian cash investments for U.S. cash investments. The U.S. economy is about ten times the size of the Canadian economy, and therefore the U.S. currency has more purchasing power on the world market. Therefore, the transfer to U.S. cash investments was a good move, because it guaranteed the purchasing power of their savings. However, the timing of the strategy created a problem. People waited until a day or two before the referendum to convert their Canadian cash investments to U.S. cash investments. The market usually reflects the same concerns we have. In this case, it made the conversion more expensive.

What did I do just before the referendum? Nothing. For many years, I had placed my money in shares of Coca-Cola, Merck, Bristol Myers and Intel, all U.S. companies. My RRSPs were invested in Canadian companies such as Bombardier and Seagram. The Canadian sales of these two companies account for less than 10% of their total sales. Therefore, if something had happened between Quebec and Canada, it would have had little impact on the value of their shares.

Here is another personal example that I vividly recall. A few years ago, the Mexican peso lost 40% of its value in one day. There was some talk at the time that the Canadian dollar was going to be devalued next. Imagine if the

Canadian dollar lost 40% of its value in one day! Would the loonie be considered a safe investment, even with the usual government guarantee on term deposits? To many people the answer is yes. However, this guarantee only protects the amount of the original investment. It does not protect its purchasing power for imported goods. When I heard the news about this run on the peso, I recall not being the least bit concerned. As mentioned earlier, most of my investments were in U.S. and international-type companies. Regardless of what happens to the Canadian dollar, these investments always maintain their purchasing power for world goods.

Risk & Predictability

I believe many people confuse risk with predictability. For example, if a bank offers 6% interest on a cash investment, it is very predictable how much we are going to earn. We see this as being risk free. But with a stock, we tend to think of it as being risky, because its growth is unpredictable (even though it may grow by more than 6%). Historically, stocks held for a long time have returned more than cash investments, although stocks are not as predictable in the short term. However, you <u>are</u> growing your wealth over a long period of time. You may begin at age 30, and continue well into your twilight years. Some people may start even earlier, which means the money could be invested for more than 50 years before it is used.

An article by Roger E. Alcaly supports the fact that, in the past, stocks have clearly outperformed cash investments.[16] This superior performance occurred over 60% of the time if stocks were held one year, 70% if held five years, 80% if held 10 years, and 90% if held 20 years. The evidence clearly indicates that the longer you hold on to your invest-

---

[16] Investor's Digest of Canada, September 11, 1998.

ment, the greater are the odds that stocks outperform cash investments. Therefore, the longer stocks are held, the lower the risk.

One question I am frequently asked when recommending stocks as an investment option is "but what about the crash of 1929?" This event is another example of people being 'probability blind'. It is similar to someone not going on a cruise ship because they remember the Titanic. Here are the facts according to Roger Alcaly. The S&P 500 index has averaged an annual rate of return of 11% from 1926-1980. This includes 1929. Where else could such returns have been made? (Roger Alcaly also points out in this article that the annual rate of return after 1980 averaged about 18%.)

Jeremy Siegel, a professor at the Wharton School of the University of Pennsylvania, wrote the book "Stocks for the Long Run". In this book, he reviewed the average rate of return for a representative group of stocks from 1802 to 1997. His research clearly documents their superior return when compared to alternatives.

The rates of return shown in the following table are adjusted for inflation. This is a very fair and meaningful way of showing figures over a long period of time.

Average Rate of Return (%)				
Start Date	Item	Start Value	Rate of Return	Value 1997
1802	Gold	$1.00	Minus 0.09%	$0.84
1802	Short Term Interest	$1.00	2.9%	$275.00
1802	Long Term Interest	$1.00	3.5%	$803.00
1802	Stocks	$1.00	7.0%	$559,000.00

The first finding that really jumps out at me is the return (really the lack thereof) on gold. Many people believe that investment in gold is very safe. Jeremy Siegel's research appears to indicate that gold has been very risky. The purchasing power of gold did not even keep up with inflation. The other really startling fact is how well stocks did.

I used to think that once my stock investments grew to a target value that I had set, I would put the entire sum into GICs. I wanted the investment to be 'safe'. However, when the time came, I had started following the philosophy outlined in this book. I did not put the money into GICs, but left the entire amount in stocks.

Today, our investments are 11 times the amount I set as the target. I share this information with you to illustrate how my thinking has evolved. I feel highly trained in the field of finance, spend most of my workday in this area, and have taken many advanced courses on risk management. Still, I am not entirely sure that I have the definitive answer to "What is risk?" I do know that my views about what is risky have changed greatly over the past few years.

My portfolio would not have grown the way it did if I had been in cash investments, instead of stocks. In 1985, Wrigley, a gum company, was trading between $3 and $5 per share. Recently the price was $70. It is almost inconceivable that the price would ever fall back to anything near the $3-$5 range. So is it a good time to buy this stock? I don't know. However, I do know that the Russian and Chinese markets have opened up to Wrigley products in a manner that just a few years ago would have seemed impossible. The company has no debt, and the outlook is as good today as it ever was. We are talking about a product, gum, that my son claims was invented 3,000 years ago by the Chinese. You don't always need bright new ideas or complex hi-tech schemes to make money. I like to own the shares of companies that sell things that go into our mouths and are consumed. This leaves room for more sales.

Remember our bathtub analogy, where your savings are represented by the amount of water left in the tub. The water coming through the faucet represents income from your job, and the drain represents your spending. If you want more money, you must invest your savings wisely. How do you decide what to do? The volatility of the market leads people to believe that stocks are risky, and therefore they choose cash investments. However, cash investments, while very predictable, do not provide a good rate of return. Stocks actually reduce financial risk, because they have a better rate of return. In the long run, volatility is not relevant.

CASH INVESTMENTS

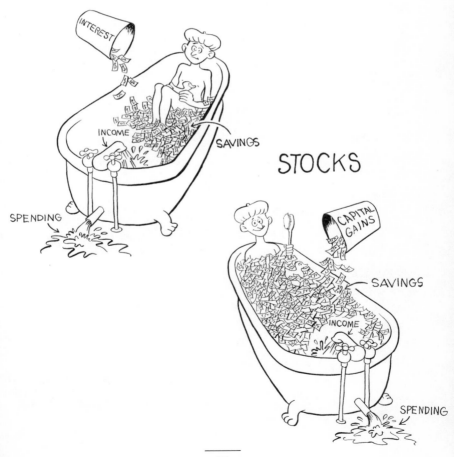

STOCKS

Summary

Do you know the average rate of return of your investments for each of the last three years? (To review how to do this, see "Keeping It Simple - Investments" in Chapter 3, "The Basics".) Anyone who cannot answer this question is probably not a logical investor. We must base our investment decisions on statistical data, instead of gut feel. (Remember our 'probability blind' limitation.) Decisions based on past information from your feedback system are better than decisions made at random.

Chapter 9

Income Taxes

"Anyone may so arrange his affairs that his taxes shall be as low as possible; he is not bound to choose that pattern which will best pay the treasury; there is not even a patriotic duty to increase one's taxes."

- Judge Learned Hand

Consider this. Over your lifetime, you will likely spend more on taxes than anything else. It makes sense that one of the first steps you should take in building your wealth is to understand taxes sufficiently to minimize this large cash outflow.

The following is intended to highlight the key points that you should know about taxes. It is not an in-depth tax course. Seek professional help from a chartered accountant if you need to know more. For readers who dislike numbers, I apologize. Bear with me. It will be well worth the effort.

Taxable Income

Taxable income is a defined term in the income tax act. It is the amount of income on which we must pay taxes. Not all income is taxed equally, and some is not taxed at all. What is really important from a decision point of view, however, is our current marginal tax rate.

Marginal Tax Rates

Your marginal tax rate is based on your taxable income.

It represents the combined effect of both the federal and the provincial income taxes. The following table explains how marginal tax rates work. It is based on calculations using the Ontario provincial tax rate, but the tax rates of the other provinces are similar. Please note that I have rounded the figures.

Marginal Tax Rate	
Taxable Income	Marginal Tax Rate
$ 0 - 6,500	0%
$ 6,500 - 30,000	26%
$30,000 - 60,000	41%
$60,000 and above	52%

The following graph provides a more visual depiction of this same information.

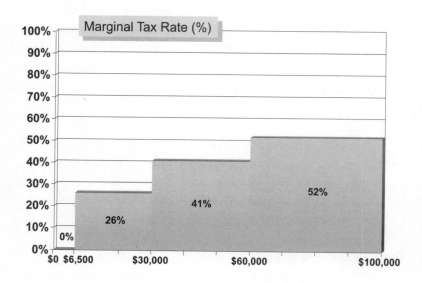

Let's look at this more closely. If you earn less than $6,500, you pay no taxes. If you earn more than $6,500 but less than $30,000, you pay no taxes on the first $6,500, and keep 74 cents of each dollar earned between $6,500 and $30,000 (and our governments keep the remaining 26 cents). If your annual income is greater than $30,000 and less than $60,000, you pay no taxes on the first $6,500, keep 74 cents of each dollar earned between $6,500 and $30,000, and keep 59 cents of every dollar earned between $30,000 and $60,000. Finally, if you earn more than $60,000 annually, you pay no taxes on the first $6,500, keep 74 cents of each dollar earned between $6,500 and $30,000, keep 59 cents of every dollar earned between $30,000 and $60,000, and keep 48 cents of every dollar earned beyond $60,000.

Contrary to popular belief, you never lose money by moving into a higher tax bracket. You always gain something by earning another dollar. Yes, as you move up into higher marginal tax rates, the government does take a higher percentage; above $60,000 the government actually takes 52% (you still keep 48%). However, for every dollar up to $60,000 of taxable income, you keep the larger share.

The following graph depicts the total amount of taxes paid on taxable income up to $100,000.

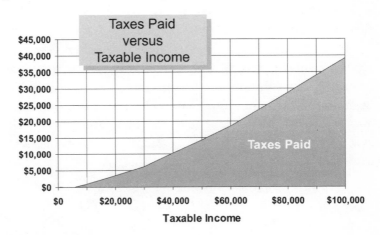

85

To find out how much tax you pay, find your taxable income on the bottom axis. Then move up until you hit the top of the 'taxes paid' area. Read across to the vertical axis on the left to see how much tax you pay. For example, at $40,000 of taxable income, expect a tax bill of about $10,000. Please note that this does not include what you pay in Canada Pension Plan or Employment Insurance.

The key to understanding taxes for investment purposes is to be aware of the top marginal tax rate into which you fall. This is the only relevant rate to use for all investment and tax planning.

Why is this important? You can minimize the taxes you pay by arranging and controlling your financial affairs. The marginal tax data provides the numbers required for the calculations.

Let's look at RRSPs. When you buy one, it lowers your taxable income; when you cash it in, it increases your taxable income. It would not be wise to buy an RRSP when your taxable income was less than $6,500, because your marginal tax rate is zero. (Since you don't owe taxes anyway, there would be no tax savings at the time you buy the RRSP.) However, if you had bought an RRSP when your income was less than $6,500, you would owe taxes on this money when you cash it in, if your taxable income at that time was above $6,500.

If your income was more than $60,000 when you purchased an RRSP, you would save 52% (your marginal tax rate) at the time the amount was invested. When you cash it in during retirement, your marginal tax rate will likely be less (e.g. 41%) due to your lower income. Hence, you will pay 11% less tax (52% - 41%), and have the benefits of growth!

Tax Exemptions

Calculating how much income tax you must pay at a certain income level is only part of the equation. You must also look at <u>what</u> is taxed.

Certain items, such as the profit made on your principal residence, are not taxed. Profit is defined as the difference between the purchase price and the selling price. This income is tax-exempt, even if it is millions of dollars. I have seen some clients make enough for a comfortable retirement from the tax-free profit on the sale of their home.

Now let's look at capital gains. (This is the amount that a share has increased in value from the time that you purchased it, to the time that you sell it.) Only 75% of capital gains are taxed, leaving the other 25% tax-free. Therefore, if you are in the top tax bracket and receive $1,000 as a salary increase or as interest income from cash investments, the government will take 52% or $520. You will keep only $480. But if you receive a capital gain of $1,000, you will only be taxed on 75% of it, or on $750. In this case, the government takes $390 (52% of $750), and you keep $610. Therefore, you will save $130 ($610 - $480). This is a saving of 13% after tax, which is equivalent to about 26% before tax. This is a very substantial benefit! Convert a cash investment (e.g. term deposit) into shares, and you will receive this tax break, as well as the probability of a higher return.

Tax-Deferred Items

The next best thing to not paying taxes is to delay their payment (defer taxes). The longer you can defer them, the better. This is a good idea for two reasons. First, you can use this deferred tax money to earn investment income. Second, taxation of the income can be delayed until your marginal tax rate is lower (e.g. when you are retired).

For the average person, shares provide the best vehicle to accomplish this feat. Taxes are only paid on capital gains at the time the shares are sold, whereas with interest-bearing cash investments, tax is paid annually. This is a great tax-planning opportunity. Next to RRSPs, it is probably the biggest tax break that is available to Canadians. Let's look at an actual example.

Suppose that you had a $100,000 term deposit invested at 8% interest, and that you are taxed at the top marginal rate. The tax bite of 52% on the $8,000 interest earned each year would be $4,160, leaving you with $3,840. Now instead of this $100,000 being on deposit at the Royal Bank, let us assume that you bought $100,000 worth of Royal Bank shares. If during the past year, the shares actually doubled in price, your $100,000 would now be worth $200,000! However, you wouldn't owe any taxes until the shares are sold. The tax to be paid will be determined by your income at that time. Therefore, you could plan to sell the shares when you don't have much income. Remember, only 75% of the $100,000 capital gain is included in taxable income when the shares are cashed.

Now, as a shareholder, let us assume you need $4,000 cash at the end of the year. You would sell $5,000 worth of stock. Since the stock had doubled in value, this $5,000 from the sale is composed of $2,500 of your original principal, plus $2,500 capital gain. Only the capital gain portion is taxable. As mentioned before, only 75% of this $2,500 (or $1,875) is included as taxable income. The taxes owing are $975 (52% of $1,875), leaving you with remaining cash of $4,025 ($5000 - $975) and $195,000 in stock. Remember, if you had invested in the term deposit, you would only have $3,840 in cash (after paying tax on interest earned for the year) and $100,000 in the term deposit.

Isn't it fascinating how much our wealth can increase, and how easily we can get our hands on the cash we need, without paying much in taxes? We have just touched on some very important points. Yes, it was unusual to have shares double so quickly. However, the chance for them to increase was there. There was no chance for the term deposit to double. Even if the shares had made only modest gains, the key point is that the tax act treats capital gains more favorably than interest.

Income Splitting

Income splitting is a very important strategy in tax planning. Imagine a family where a husband and wife have a combined income of $60,000. If only one person earned this income, the income taxes owing are $17,600. But if each person earned $30,000 instead of one earning $60,000 and the other nothing, their combined tax bill would be only $12,800. This is a tax saving of $4,800. The couple on one income is paying 37.5% more taxes than the couple with two incomes. The one-income family would have to earn $9,600 more than the two-income family to have the same after-tax income. That is a lot of money.

There are two areas where income splitting can be used effectively. The first is available only to the self employed. Instead of a sole proprietorship, you form a partnership with your spouse. In a partnership, income can be split with your partner. If the business is incorporated, each may take out a salary as long as both spouses actually work in the business. If the children are actively employed in the business, you may pay them a fair wage for work done. These are opportunities that simply aren't available to people who aren't self-employed.

The second opportunity to income split is with investment earnings. For those investments outside an RRSP, the spouse with the lowest income should have all of the couple's investments in that name, thereby claiming all of their investment income. This method permits investment income to be earned and taxed in the hands of the person with the lowest marginal tax rate. This saves taxes.

However, for investments inside RRSPs, the spouse earning the highest income should buy their maximum before the other spouse buys any. As will be discussed in Chapter 10, "RRSPs", by planning and using the 'spousal' RRSP option, you and your spouse will have equal incomes on retirement. From a tax planning point of view, this is as good as it gets.

There is much made in the financial papers of this opportunity to split income. It makes logical sense to have interest income earned by the spouse with the lowest marginal tax rate. However, it is even better if both of them avoid earning interest income altogether, by having all of their investments in shares. This way they get the benefit of appreciating stock value, without having to pay an annual tax on their increase in wealth. They can defer paying taxes until they need the money and sell their stocks.

Canada Pension Plan benefits offer another opportunity to split income, with the full blessing of Revenue Canada. If both spouses are over the age of 60, up to half the CPP benefit that one spouse receives may be assigned to the other spouse, so that the total CPP income received is split equally between the two. Attribution rules (tax laws designed to prevent income splitting) do not apply to the assignment of CPP benefits. It is hard to go wrong by taking advantage of this generous offer by Revenue Canada.

Company pensions usually cannot be shared or split. However, most companies allow a continuity option. As mentioned before, the retiring person takes a slightly lower pension from the start of retirement, but at his death, his pension continues to be paid to his spouse. Without the continuation option, the pension would terminate at the death of the pensioner, without any provision for his partner. Most people should seriously consider the continuation option. It provides more financial security to the partner without the pension.

Claw Backs

The annual Old Age Security (OAS) for people over 65 is $4,847. If you earn more than $53,215, then 15% of any amount above $53,215 is clawed back.[17] In other words, it is a big claw.

Income splitting has a great impact with respect to claw backs. If two people earn $50,000 each, there is no claw back on the OAS received. If one spouse earns $70,000 and the other $30,000, the spouse with the $70,000 income is subject to a claw back. Let's look at the figures. The amount of income in excess of the base amount is $16,785 ($70,000-$53,215). The OAS claw back amounts to 15% of $16,785 or about $2,518. That is a lot of extra taxes to pay.
That's why it is important to arrange your affairs so that the tax bite is minimized.

Employment Insurance (EI), not to be outdone, is also subject to claw back. The base amount for EI is $39,000 and the rate of claw back is 30% of all amounts above this base! This is an even bigger claw.

One may wonder how someone collecting Employment Insurance could earn enough income to be subject to a claw back. The answer is that the person may have received a severance package, started a new job, or realized a capital gain from selling the family cottage.

---

[17] Based on 1997 tax figures.

Corporate Taxes

There is a very substantial tax break available to people who are able to incorporate. The corporate tax rate, especially for small Canadian owned corporations, is considerably less than the personal tax rate. Let me explain.

Let's assume you run a successful business that generates an annual taxable income of $200,000. You would pay approximately $91,210 in personal income taxes. For those of you who love numbers, here is how it breaks down. On the first $6,500 of this $200,000 of income, you pay no tax. On the next $23,500, you pay taxes at the rate of 26% or $6,110. The tax rate is 41% on the next $30,000 or $12,300. The tax rate is 52% or $72,800 on the remaining $140,000. There is no way to legally avoid paying these taxes except by sheltering some of this income through RRSPs.

Now let's look at how much tax you would pay if you 'incorporated' this business. A corporation is a concept whereby your business becomes a legal person in the eyes of the taxman. (It will cost you about $1,000 to incorporate.) The corporation files its own tax return, totally separate from you the owner. The key point is that now your corporation will pay tax on this income, not you. The corporation pays a flat rate of only 23% on the first $200,000 of income each year. Using the above example, the taxes owing would drop from $91,000 to $46,000.

Should you require a salary to live on, your corporation can pay you one. This salary is considered to be an expense to the corporation, thus lowering its income and therefore its tax. However, this salary would now be taxable to you the individual.

If you own the corporation, you are a shareholder. Therefore, you may also obtain money from your corporation by having it pay you a dividend (a pay out of a corporation's earnings to its shareholders). For the individual, these dividends are taxed at a lower rate than is salary. However, dividends (unlike salary) are not a deductible expense for the corporation. Therefore, once you combine the taxes you pay as an individual with those paid by your corporation, there is little overall advantage to paying dividends instead of salary.

If the owner requires all the earnings of his business to live on, then incorporation does not provide a tax break, as the corporation will have zero income. These earnings would be taxed in his hands as salary, just as if he had not incorporated. The only tax advantage of incorporating is when income is left in the corporation.

Due to the corporation's lower tax rate, a lot more money is left to invest. The corporation can make the same investments as can an individual. This is another opportunity to grow your money.

As a point of interest, my public practice is not incorporated. Accountants, lawyers, doctors and dentists are not permitted to incorporate in Ontario. However, I certainly would incorporate, if I was allowed to do so.

Super Exemption

There is a really huge tax break that the accounting industry fondly refers to as 'the super exemption.' If you own shares of your own corporation, you may sell your shares for up to $500,000 more than you paid for them, and not pay any income tax.[18] If your spouse owns half the shares of this company with you, then together you can make a million-dollar gain and not pay any income taxes! I cannot understand why this exemption exists. Should successful people pay no taxes on half a million dollars of

---

[18] The company must be a Canadian-controlled private corporation engaged in active business. There may be an alternative minimum tax payable. However, this tax is refundable in future years.

income, while an office worker earning about $20,000 has a substantial tax bill?

If you want a lot of tax-free money, go for this super exemption. To do it, you need a good idea that turns into a profitable business. Once you have that, incorporate and then sell your shares for up to $500,000 more than your cost. It is not easy, but the tax breaks available are truly incredible. A farmer enjoys the same tax break. He can sell his farm for $500,000 more than he paid for it ($1,000,000 more if owned jointly) and he will not pay any taxes. In order to qualify for the super exemption, you must adhere to certain rules. These requirements are not onerous. However, to be on the safe side, call your accountant.

It is amazing how much tax you can save or defer by simply rearranging your affairs. You can now understand why I love to discuss taxes with my clients. I am reminded of a joke that states "accountants are not boring people, they just get excited about boring things."

ACCOUNTANTS ARE NOT BORING PEOPLE, THEY JUST GET EXCITED ABOUT BORING THINGS!

Chapter 10

RRSPs

An RRSP is a government incentive that encourages saving for retirement. The RRSP contribution lowers your taxable income. You save your marginal tax rate (26%, 41% or 52%) on the amount that is contributed at the time, and receive this refund immediately when you file your tax return.[19] Also, you pay absolutely no tax on the earnings made inside the RRSP, as long as you do not withdraw them. Once you do take out money from an RRSP, you are taxed at your marginal rate on all funds withdrawn, regardless if it is principal or interest.

The amount you may shelter (i.e. defer from the payment of taxes) each year is limited by the 'RRSP room' you have. This amount is the lesser of either 18% of your earned income (income from employment, rentals and self-employment) or $13,500 annually, whichever is less. If you have a pension plan, the amount your employer has contributed to it is deducted from your available 'room'. RRSP deductions not used one year may be carried forward and used in subsequent years. There is a seven-year limitation to the carry forward.

RRSPs are long term investments. It is therefore important to obtain a high rate of return from them. Most people know that GICs, term deposits, savings accounts and mutu-

---

[19] Suppose you earn $30,000. Your employer deducts tax from your paycheck. Your $1,000 RRSP lowers your taxable income to $29,000. Your RRSP refund is really a refund of taxes you have already paid on this $1,000.

al funds are allowed in RRSPs. However, many people are not aware that shares are also permitted. I personally prefer to hold shares, and nothing else, in my RRSPs. Whatever you hold in your RRSP, the foreign content of it must be limited to 20% of the amount in that specific RRSP plan. By definition, 'foreign' means corporations whose head offices are not in Canada (for equity investments), and all non-Canadian dollar deposits (for cash type investments).

To open an RRSP plan (account), go to a discount broker, full service broker, or a bank, and sign some forms. A 'self-administered' plan is the only way to hold shares in an RRSP. It also allows you to hold all the other RRSP investments permitted. It costs about $125 annually. I like this type of plan, because all your RRSP investments can be in just one place. This helps to keep things simple. Also, by having just one account, it is easier to keep track of your RRSP foreign content. The limit of 20% applies to each account you have. Therefore, if you hold two RRSP accounts and have only taken 10% foreign content on one of them, you cannot make it up by taking 30% on the other one.

To illustrate the value of saving and using RRSPs, consider the following example. Let's assume that two people, John and Joan, each earn $35,000 a year. Each manages to save $6.50 every day ($2,370 annually). They each invest this amount, and earn 10% interest per year. Joan, unlike John, decides to buy an RRSP. She knows that she will get a tax refund by doing this. So, she takes out a loan in the amount of the tax refund that she expects back i.e. $1,630. Therefore, she invests $4,000 in her RRSP ($2,370 of savings + $1,630 from the loan). When she files her tax return, the government will refund her $1,640 (marginal tax rate of 41% x $4,000). She uses this refund to pay back the bank for the $1,630 borrowed. (Less than a month should elapse from the time she borrows the money to the time she obtains her tax refund.) Joan, by investing the $1,630 extra from her tax saving, is investing 69% more money each year than is John!

It gets even better when you consider the impact of interest. The government will defer taxing any interest earned by Joan's investment until the funds are withdrawn from her RRSP. This means that all the interest earned can be added to the investment base, allowing for its rapid growth. Meanwhile, John pays taxes of 41% annually on the interest earned by his $2,370, and reinvests only the remaining amount.

Let's look at RRSPs this way. If you put your money into a special bank account called RRSP instead of a regular bank account, the government (other taxpayers) will give you back about half the money you invested. The only catch is that some day, perhaps 30 years later, you will have to pay taxes on the funds withdrawn. In effect, an RRSP is a transfer of money from taxpayers who do not save to those that do. Make no mistake about it. RRSPs present one of the biggest tax loopholes available to Canadians. Everyone should take advantage of the RRSP opportunity before some government takes it away. In some ways, I find it hard to believe such a generous tax break still exists.

The following graph is a comparison of Joan and John's results after saving $6.50 a day for 30 years. The interest rate earned throughout the period for both was assumed to be 10%.[20]

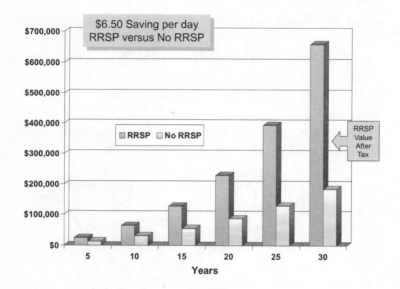

After 30 years, John accumulated $184,103 after tax! Joan, the RRSP person, has accumulated $657,976! At this point, if they both cashed in their savings, Joan would lose $328,988 (50% of $657,976) to taxes, while John would not lose any. However, even after the impact of taxes, Joan has accumulated $328,988. This is $144,885 more than John has managed to save!

---

[20] The rate of 10% was picked because I felt it was achievable. The appendix has the year by year figures for 8%, 10% 12%, and 18%.

RRSPs offer another advantage to married people. The government allows you to buy an RRSP in either your name, or your spouse's name (spousal RRSP). In either case, you receive the same immediate benefit of a reduction in your taxable income. For example, if you are married and your spouse has a lower taxable income, or does not work outside the home, buy a portion of the RRSPs in your name and the balance as a spousal RRSP (your deduction but registered in your spouse's name). The reason for doing this is so that when you and your spouse withdraw money from these RRSPs during retirement, you will be minimizing the amount taxed at the top marginal rate. You will each have a small amount of taxes to pay (at the lower  marginal tax rate), as opposed to one spouse paying a lot and the other one paying very little. As much as possible, plan to equalize incomes (including pensions) on retirement. Spousal RRSPs provide a vehicle to make this happen.

Remember that another advantage of RRSPs is that upon the death of one spouse, the RRSP money may be transferred - tax free - to the survivor. If this were not so, there would be an immediate tax burden. Only when the surviving spouse dies must taxes finally be paid.

When should you withdraw some money from your RRSP? Not until you require it. Withdraw only the amount that you need to live on, keeping the bulk of it tax sheltered. At age 69, you must close your RRSP. At this point, I recommend converting an RRSP into a RRIF (Registered Retirement Income Fund).

A RRIF is just an RRSP with one more condition attached. This condition requires that you must take out a certain amount each year, like it or not. At age 70, you must withdraw 4.7% of the previous year's ending balance. This rises to 20% of the previous year's balance at age 94, and remains at this rate thereafter. You may also take out more (but not less) than the minimum amount prescribed by the RRIF.

My experience is that it is best not to change the RRSP into a RRIF before it is necessary. There is one exception. Revenue Canada allows taxpayers who are 65 or older to receive $1,000 of annual pension income tax-free. To obtain this deduction, you must have at least this amount as pension income. If no pension income exists, you can create some by changing some of your RRSP to a RRIF, and then withdrawing $1,000 annually out of the RRIF. Why this tax deduction is allowed or how long it will last is anyone's guess. Why should a poor person who is left with just a bit of interest income get less of a tax break than a person left with a big pension?

I'd like to conclude with some statistics. A Gallup survey of more than 1,000 adults found that, "Canadians, by and large, are dangerously ignorant about their finances."[21] These are very strong words. The survey found that only 44% could define inflation correctly as "when things go up in price" or something close to this definition. Only 59% of respondents knew about stocks, and just 22% knew about mutual funds. Fewer than 50% were even aware of RRSPs! Given the massive ads released every winter, the author rightly wondered, "Where are Canadians hiding?"

Here is more data from that study. Only 1% of the people surveyed saved more than $10,000 annually. Only 20% of those who contributed to an RRSP kept track of the

---

[21] An article entitled Net Worth by Anne Kingston.

amount they bought! I found this information very surprising. It is important to know how much you've invested, what it's invested in, and how well it is doing. As I've said before, I like keeping score of how my investments are doing compared to the market. I want to know the facts in order to improve future performance.

A 1995 review by Statistics Canada found that the unused RRSP room in Canada was $133 billion.[22] Canadians had saved only 16.5% of what they were allowed in this fantastic tax break. The average RRSP (total value held) at the start of 1995 was $30,000.

Registered Retirement Savings Plans (RRSPs) are one of the most effective strategies you can utilize to grow your wealth. They provide many people with the opportunity to save about twice the amount of money (and own the resulting growth), as compared to someone who does not take advantage of them! If you have room to buy RRSPs, and are not taking full advantage of it, you should seriously examine your strategy. If you have any doubt as to how much you are allowed to buy, check the assessment that you received from Revenue Canada, or give them a call. They are very helpful people.

---

[22] The Globe and Mail, December 7, 1995.

Chapter 11

Insurance

Insurance is based on the premise that we will accept a small immediate loss (the premium) to protect ourselves against a potential larger loss (the peril).

There are three basic insurance categories - life, disability and casualty. Life insurance pays money to your estate if you die. Disability insurance provides you with some money if you are no longer able to earn all, or a portion of, your income. Casualty insurance pays for loss or damage to your property (including house and automobile).

Why should you have insurance? To protect yourself from a big financial hit, especially if this would cause a lot of hardship. When should you not have insurance? When there is nothing to protect, or when you can afford to take the financial hit.

Life Insurance

If you are the sole breadwinner for a family, have two young children at home, are not independently wealthy, and do not have term life insurance, then you are likely making a mistake. There is a definite need for life insurance in many situations. However, as I have said before, I do not recommend whole-life insurance which mixes insurance with investing. There are better methods to grow your money. Buy only term insurance (a policy that is not linked to investing) and only the amount you need. Also, shop around to compare your cost. I was recently mailed a fancy brochure, promoting great life insurance rates. It advertised a cost of only $119 annually for $100,0000 of coverage (male non-smoker under 35). I can get the same $100,000 coverage through the Chartered Accountants of Ontario for $72. The advertised 'great deal' cost 65% more!

Keep in mind that once you purchase an insurance policy, you will not likely review it regularly. Therefore, not only is it important to get the best price you can for the insurance, you should also make sure that you choose the correct policy. Let's look at some areas where your life insurance needs should be examined.

Life insurance does not make a lot of sense if you are a single person with no dependents. You are paying to get something only if you die. This is not my cup of tea. I know of a young single woman who owed a lot on a student loan. She was paying $480 annually in life insurance premiums. (Her mother and grandmother had each taken out a policy on her as well.) It would have been much better if the money used for insurance had been used to pay down her student loan.

It also makes no sense to insure a child. If a child dies, there is no income lost, as in the case of the family breadwinner. A child who dies does not benefit from the insurance payoff. If the child lives, the premiums are wasted. This child would be much better off if the money was invested in trust for her.

death of a taxpayer with money in a RRIF and
spouse, the entire balance left in this account
ıble income. For example, the estate of someone
)0 left in a RRIF can expect to pay about $100,000
),000). This tax cannot be avoided. The more that
ıs ı..   ̣e RRIF, the bigger the tax payment. Life insurance
companies see this as a great opportunity to sell policies to
cover the cost of taxes. However, I don't feel these policies
are necessary. First, there is no financial risk to be covered.
The estate is simply paying taxes that have been deferred
for a long time. Second, the estate would have been worth
more, if the money used to pay for insurance had instead
been invested in TIPS or SPYDERS.

Banks are eager to sell loan life insurance to anyone who
takes out a loan or mortgage. If you die, the balance of the
loan is paid off. Loan insurance provides the bank with a
guaranteed loan payment if the policyholder dies, and if the
policyholder lives, the bank pockets the profits from the
premiums. It is great for their business. I never buy this loan
insurance and this is why. When you take out a loan to buy
an asset (and remember that you should not take out a loan
to 'buy' an expense), you do not incur added risk. You still
have the asset, which can be sold to pay off the loan.
Therefore, there is no need for insurance.

How does the cost of loan life insurance compare to that
of term life insurance? I phoned my banker to get the bank's
rates for loan life insurance for someone under 35 years old.
For $100,000 it is $216 annually. This is 200% more than the
$72 discussed earlier for the same coverage with term life
insurance! Remember to buy only what you need.

I don't recommend buying life insurance for accidental
death. The odds of accidental death are very low. Consider
this. Does your estate need any less money if you die of a
heart attack (not an accident) instead of an airplane crash?

Make sure that you are insured for all types of death, not just accidental death. All things considered, this insurance is probably the most expensive insurance you can buy.

Disability Insurance

Disability insurance is a very common benefit to employees of medium and large companies. However, most self-employed people, or those working for small companies, do not have this coverage. The reason for this is that the premiums for this coverage are substantial. However, the need is there. Statistics show that the probability of a 30-year-old having a long-term disability is much higher than the probability of him dying.[23] It can be a more onerous financial burden to the family for the main wage earner to become disabled than to die. The disabled person may require full-time care, and this can put the surviving partner in a precarious financial situation.

The most important feature of any disability insurance contract is the definition of 'disability'. This provision determines when you are considered disabled for the purpose of collecting benefits.

As outlined in the "Personal Financial Planner's Manual" published by the Canadian Institute of Chartered Accountants (CICA), there are three varieties of the definition in common use: 'any occupation', 'own occupation', and 'split definition.' 'Any occupation' defines disability as "the complete inability of the insured to engage in any occupation whatsoever." This approach is rather strict. Insurers have recently defined 'any occupation' as the "complete inability of the insured to engage in gainful occupation for which he (she) is or becomes reasonably fitted by education, training or experience," or some similar wording. This is the

---

[23] Information supplied by The Mutual Group.

least liberal as far as the consumer is concerned, because it is the most difficult to collect if you become disabled. For example, if you are a doctor and become so disabled that you can no longer practice medicine but are able to pump gas, you are not disabled by this definition. Avoid the 'any occupation' type of disability insurance, if you can.

'Own occupation' means "prevented by such disability from performing the important duties pertaining to the employee's occupation." This is the most liberal approach from the consumers' viewpoint. It also means this insurance is the most expensive. Go for it, if you can afford it.

'Split definition' is a combination of the two previous types. In this policy, total disability may mean "complete inability of the insured to engage in any gainful occupation for which he or she is reasonably fitted by education, training or experience. However, during the first 24 months of any period of disability, the insurer will deem the insured to be totally disabled if he or she is unable to engage in his or her own occupation."

Review your disability insurance to be certain that it provides adequate coverage.

Casualty Insurance

People are most familiar with casualty insurance. For example, most of us have fire, theft, and third party liability insurance on our homes, apartments and vehicles. I feel it would be foolish not to have this insurance. Buy adequate coverage, but shop around for it. It is my experience that the premiums vary as much for casualty insurance as they do for life insurance.

There are several ways of saving money on casualty insurance - money that you can then use to invest. First, be careful not to over-insure. For example, do not buy collision insurance on an old vehicle. Second, consider increasing your various deductibles (the amount that you personally pay before the insurance coverage kicks in).

In the casualty insurance area, it rarely pays to buy an extended warranty for an appliance. Companies want to sell this insurance, because such sales are highly profitable for them. Recently, I bought a $55 electronic scheduler for my son. The sales clerk really wanted to sell me two years of extended warranty insurance for $9. This is the way I looked at it. An electronic item such as a scheduler rarely breaks down. The manufacturer already covers this product against defects for a period of three months. Buying it with my gold credit card automatically doubles the length of warranty on it for up to an additional year. If the electronic product works fine for the first six months of use, what are the chances of its breaking down within the next 18 months? The $9 of insurance is 16% of the original price. I didn't feel the cost was worth it.

The other day I picked up a video for our family to watch and was asked if I wanted to pay 25 cents for tape protection. This insurance only covers damage done to the tape by your VCR. It does not cover other accidents, such as your dog chewing up the tape. I declined tape protection, because I felt I could handle the cost of replacing a tape in the unlikely event of it being damaged. (The cost of a new tape, depending on whether it is an old or new release, varies from $9 to $100.)

An option which can be used in place of casualty insurance is self-insurance. This is when you put aside, perhaps in a special account, the money you would have paid in premiums. Money is available from this account when an accident occurs. It may make sense to self-insure, if you already have a sizeable net worth and/or sufficient cash flow to handle the loss. Long term, the probability is that you will be money ahead by using self-insurance, because you are not paying an insurance company to handle it. However, there is a risk involved. You must decide if the potential gain outweighs the risk.

Summary
Carefully examine your insurance needs, and determine the coverage that you require. Shop around to get the best rate. Make sure that you ask for standard deductions that you can get for being a non-smoker, a senior citizen, or having no prior claims. Paying more than you should for this expense can amount to a large sum.

Chapter 12

Investing Is Like Marriage

A few years ago, I came to the realization that investing is like marriage. Now I use the marriage analogy to verify whether or not my investment strategy makes sense. When you think about it, picking the right life partner is one of the most important decisions we make. The initial step we take is to get to know the person firsthand, and we do this by spending a lot of time with him or her. Note how different this is from the way we usually select investments. We rely on tips, read newspapers and review reports. Why do we pick our partner ourselves, instead of hiring an expert or team of experts to do this for us? For decisions that are truly important to us, we trust no one but ourselves. I believe that in the same way we trust ourselves to pick our partner, we should trust our judgment in choosing companies to invest in.

As in choosing a partner, the first step in choosing a company is to get to know it well. (This is explained in Chapter 13, "Finding Value".) If the quality of the company's management is so high that it really excites you, then and only then is it time to examine the company's financial aspects. Likewise, we would not check out a person's wealth before we had the first date.

If you are really enamoured with how well a company is managed, do not be afraid to make a very significant investment in it. This can be likened to the significant step of marriage (to a single individual). If you are not 'in love' with a company, then do not invest. Keep your money in participation units such as TIPS and SPYDERS.

Trying to time when to buy a stock makes as much sense as trying to time when to get married. The key is not when, but with whom. Selection is everything. Let's look at what would have happened if, in 1982, you 'married' Coke U.S. as an investment. The cost per share then was $1.50. By June 1998, it was worth $85. The increase was even greater due to the devaluation of the Canadian dollar from $.90 to $.68 during that time. The point is that you had to 'marry it', instead of guessing when to buy and/or sell it.

Diversification of investments is generally accepted as a cornerstone of good financial planning. My experience has taught me otherwise, as the wealthiest people I know have diversified the least. If we go back to the marriage analogy, we would not think to diversify by marrying many spouses. This point may be a little off the wall, but I am trying to get across a very critical concept. The more we diversify, the more we are choosing against our 'first love'. Assume you had one week to pick 100 spouses. How fussy would you be about who your spouses were? You would not have time to be selective. Quality would not be the key issue. On the other hand, when we plan to make only one choice, and have no time limit, quality becomes all-encompassing. I believe the increased emphasis on quality actually reduces overall investment risk, in spite of the lack of diversification.

Now that I have made my point about diversification, I will relax my position somewhat. A small harem of stocks may be acceptable! In other words, you do not have to stay with only one stock. However, I do suggest that you should never have more than a dozen. By far the biggest error I have made to date is being too diversified. I did considerably better when I made the conscious decision to consolidate. Now half my investments are in just two shares! Review your own situation. How much has your money grown for you in the last five years? What would your results have been if you had put all your money in your two favorite stocks?

Warren Buffett is a famous investor, and one of the world's richest people. He is the first person to have made his fortune purely from investing. In the book "The Warren Buffett Way" by Robert Hagstrom, I read that in 1990 there were just six different stocks in the portfolio within his holding company (Berkshire Hathaway). Coca-Cola Company accounted for 40% of the value of the entire portfolio. If Warren Buffett holds only six stocks, why should you or I need more?

Trading stocks is as illogical as trading marriage partners. Marriage is, or should be, a long-term commitment. Yes, there will be ups and downs in the relationship. However, this is normal and not a reason for 'trading'. Similarly with stocks, do not make a commitment unless you are going to stay in for the long haul. Don't worry about short-term fluctuations. Warren Buffett exemplifies this strategy. He has stated that he never plans to sell his Coke shares.

Every time you trade stocks, you can lose up to 40% of your profit due to income taxes and commissions. Therefore, you are left with less to invest. Stick with the same stock, and you won't pay taxes until you sell it. Instead, cash in only the amount you require when your income stream stops. Again, this is comparable to our real life experience. 'Trade' your spouse (divorce), and you stand to lose half your assets.

Let me give you a personal example of 'falling in love' with an investment. A few years ago I attended a course on accounting software. At break, I asked the lecturer which high tech company he felt was well run. His favorite company was ATI Technologies Inc. It was listed on the Toronto Stock Exchange. I began thinking about investing in this company. I called a friend, who works in the high tech industry, to ask his advice. He didn't know much about ATI Technologies Inc. He did say, however, that if he were ever going to buy shares, his top pick would be Fonorola. (This Canadian company sells long distance telephone usage and competes against Bell Canada.) He had done a lot of work for Fonorola and in his opinion, it was the best-run company that he had ever dealt with. He told me about its history and plans. It sounded intriguing, but I needed to know more.

I took my friend to lunch to have a more in-depth discussion about Fonorola. He spoke about their very impressive track record. Sales had grown rapidly. He explained management's strategy to me. He felt that they were very action oriented, and he was most impressed with their skills. His words were, "They do more in two years than most companies just plan in that time." He expected them to quickly become the second largest reseller of long distant telephone services in Canada.

Studying their financial statements confirmed what my friend had said. I decided to buy the Fonorola shares. They were $6 each. Three years later I was forced to sell these shares for $67 to Call-Net (they made a take-over bid).

In conclusion, pick a stock very carefully and then hang on. Time is on your side when you invest in a well-managed company. The longer you hold the stock, the more your investment grows.

Chapter 13

Finding Value

"Yes, I have been lucky. But there again, I placed myself in a position to be lucky."

- A very successful investor

S uppose you are already a convert to the benefits of equity investing, and you want to invest in specific companies, instead of partic-ipation units such as TIPS  and SPYDERS. How do you go about finding value i.e. choosing investments that will really appreciate? Before we start, let me warn you that if you do not enjoy doing a lot of research, this process is probably not for you.

Assessing Management

The shares of well-managed companies are the ones that, in the long run, are the most likely to rapidly increase in value. Therefore, the quality and character of a company's management should be our number one investment criterion. But how do we assess this, when it is a difficult and imprecise science?

Look at where you work

A starting point would be to look at the company where you work. As an employee, you have excellent insight into its management. Many of my most wealthy clients could see that the company that employed them was well run. Hence, they felt confident in buying all the shares that they could afford. They did not diversify. In other words, they did not invest in companies that they did not know as well. This approach paid off handsomely for them.

Let me tell you about someone who exemplifies good management. I came to know about this man when I started to work for a very profitable manufacturing company. Although he no longer worked there, I learned that the company's success was due mainly to his influence. He had come from the U.S. head office to take on the job as President of the Canadian operation. His mission was to either shut down the local manufacturing plant, or make it into a moneymaker. He transformed a dismal, money-losing operation into a business that consistently had an annual return on equity of 40%! For anyone not familiar with these types of numbers, suffice it to say that the company's performance was outstanding. How did he do it? First, he had superb management skills. Second, he had an intuitive business sense. Third, and most important, his people skills were exemplary. He talked and listened to the people who worked for him. He knew everyone in the plant by name, ate lunch with them, and got to know their families. He earned the respect of all employees, and they in turn would do almost anything for him.

I first experienced this man's magic when he, as a retiree, returned for the company's 60th anniversary of being in Canada. That day, we all stopped work and gathered around a temporary stage specially set up on the factory floor. The company was going through rough times, accentuated by a severe Canadian recession. Some employees had been terminated, and the rest were worried that they would be next. When the factory workers caught sight of their former president, who by this time had been gone 12 years, there was one of the loudest, most spontaneous, and most loving cheers for a person that I have ever witnessed.

The employees begged him to come back. Now that is having faith in a leader! This is the type of management that I now look for prior to investing in a company.

As an employee and a potential investor, it is also important to watch for signs of poor management. One big problem in many North American companies is that they manage numbers, instead of getting real results. The following scenario illustrates this point. Suppose a company forecasts this month's sales to be $10 million. As the month end nears, sales are less than budget, so special discounts are offered to customers to entice them to buy immediately. Customers are smart - they learn that by waiting until the last week of the month, they can get a deal. All sorts of problems and costs result from management playing these number games. The company sells its products at a discount, in order to record a sale today instead of next week. The effect on the bottom line is devastating, but not immediately apparent. The whole factory works frantically to 'make the month'. Parts are rushed in and overtime is paid. The factory becomes very inefficient, and profits decline.

Another frequent tactic used by companies is to 'extend the month'. They include the sales of the first week of the coming month with this month's sales. This is a short sighted game. As an employee, you are in a good position to see these signs of poor management firsthand.

A trusted friend may also provide you with valuable insight into the company that employs him. Is he impressed with their management? Is he excited about going to work? Is the company expanding? His enthusiasm and knowledge may lead you to start doing research on this company. Your friend's comments are the next best thing to your own first hand information.

Look Around You

Look around you for a company that is a dominant player in its business sector. Examples include Coke in the beverage industry, or Microsoft in the computer software industry. Let me explain what I mean by dominant. If kindergarten children were asked where they like to spend money, they would often name the prominent players e.g. McDonald's, Disney, and Toys R Us. Dominant and well known are almost synonymous. Don't overlook the obvious. There are two good reasons why you should start your search for value by looking at these corporations. First, a company that already controls a major part of its market is obviously very competitive, and has done many things right. Second, once they are at the top, it is difficult for other companies to dislodge them. Therefore, it is highly probable that these leading corporations will make a lot of money for their shareholders.

Local companies, the ones we deal with everyday, offer another opportunity to find value. Wal-Mart, Tim Hortons, Burger-King, retail stores, gas stations, etc. are everywhere. Where do you spend your money, and why do you choose to deal with these businesses? Your expenditures are someone else's sales. Watch for an organization that consistently 'wows' you, and a lot of other customers, with their service. Are they efficient when you deal with them? Are they always busy? Is it obvious that they are making money? Are they expanding (opening up new locations)? Is this company listed on a major exchange? What do their employees think about the company they work for? (Ask them.) Are the employees very proud to be shareholders themselves? (If they are, they will be happy to share this information with you.) If you like what you see, the next step would be to study these companies' financial statements. (I will explain more about this later.) Do their overall sales confirm that what you observed locally is happening everywhere? By reviewing these questions, you have started the process of looking for opportunities.

Watch what consumers around you are doing. Is everyone wearing Nike shirts? Are a lot of farmers buying John Deere tractors? In the parking lots, do vans make up a large portion of the vehicles you see, and are half of those made by Chrysler? My ten-year-old son once told me to buy Adidas shares, because many of the children in his school were wearing this brand! Where are people spending their money? Which corporations make these products and services?

Advertising provides other clues. For instance, I noticed that companies trying to impress the public with the high quality of their computers, used advertising slogans such as "Intel chips inside" or "includes Microsoft Windows". The companies selling the computers reasoned that mentioning these brand names would have a positive impact on their sales. If these marketers liked Intel and Microsoft, then maybe you should like them also.

Media and Reports

Newspapers, radio, television, and magazines offer yet another source to find quality run companies. Daily news items may indicate well-managed businesses. Also, there are specific business programs and articles that take an in-depth look at individual companies. Why not learn from the reporters who did all this fact-finding for you?

Independent investment letters can be purchased. The authors of these make a living by first trying to identify companies that are well managed, and then selling this knowledge. One example is "Investors Digest of Canada".

Full service brokerage firms also offer research reports on corporations. Be careful though, as these reports can be overly optimistic. Many years ago, I followed the recommendation of such a report. The stock was rated as a buy with "good long range potential". Within two years, the stock stopped trading! My entire investment disappeared. (I keep these valueless shares listed on my portfolio to remind me of this mistake.) I now use such reports only as a check to see if I missed some information. I never use them as a starting point.

Intuition

I first became interested in Bombardier Inc. and Seagram Co. Ltd. as a result of intuition. (My father-in-law would call it gut feel!) Let me explain.

My wife and I were living in Montreal in 1975. We decided to take a holiday in Cuba. While we were flying to Cuba, I struck up a conversation (I talk a lot) with the Francophones seated next to us. I asked them what books they were reading. They were studying French-Spanish dictionaries. It had never once crossed my mind that we were going to a Spanish-speaking country, and that I should bring along an English-Spanish dictionary. I was embarrassed! I had assumed that the Cubans would speak English to me. The Francophones had a totally different attitude. They wanted to speak to the Cubans in their own language.

On the flight back from Cuba, I again saw my French-speaking friends, and asked them how they enjoyed their trip. They told me how some Cubans had invited them into their homes to socialize. I had not been invited into any Cuban homes! This was not an accident. My attitude toward the Cubans was different from the attitude of my Francophone friends. They, by their actions, had shown great respect for the Cubans, their language and culture. The Cubans had realized this, and had responded with like kindness. But why is this important to the discussion at hand, finding value?

Both Bombardier and Seagram are global companies, with head offices in Montreal. Canada represents a small percentage of their sales - the balance is international. I believe that because of their Quebec roots, they, like my Francophone friends on the plane, are more sensitive to how people of other cultures feel. Their top-level management will be invited into the 'business homes' of other nations. I think this gives these businesses a big advantage. Making a sale is much more complex than just having the best product and the lowest price.

Everything else I could learn about the companies pointed toward well-managed organizations. I bought shares of Bombardier and Seagram, and I am pleased with these choices.

Expanding the Search

Once you have found a company that you believe is much better managed than the average, what is the next step? You should obtain detailed information about the company. How long has the company been in business? Who are the majority shareholders? Who are the key managers e.g. the President and Vice-Presidents? How old are they? What is their education and experience? How long have they been with the company? What is their track record for creating shareholders' wealth? Are they trustworthy? Most importantly, have the top managers purchased company shares themselves? If their actions indicate that they think the company they run is not worth investing in, take note. Do not put your money in it either.

The Internet is a wonderful tool to use in gathering corporate data. By doing a search for the company's name, you can get company profiles, financial information and press releases. Also look for the 10-K report, which contains a wealth of information about U.S. companies.

You may also want to discuss a company with your broker, and obtain any in-house investment reports available. Better still, talk to the company's employees, customers and competitors.

Lastly, you may contact the company directly for information such as annual financial statements. Every stock exchange keeps an up-to-date record of the telephone numbers of all corporations listed with them. They are happy to give you the phone number for the investor service department of any corporation. Here are the stock exchange numbers:

Stock Exchange Telephone Numbers	
Exchange	**Telephone number**
Toronto	416-947-4700
Montreal	514-871-2424
Vancouver	604-689-3334
Alberta	403-974-7400
New York	212-656-2804
American	212-306-1000
NASDAQ	202-496-2500

Assessing Value

Once you are sure that the company is well managed, how do you know that the cost of the share represents good value for money? Many stock analysts look at volumes of company statistics. I really enjoy doing this too. However, this book is not a course on how to analyze a company's financial statements. That takes years of study. What I want to share with you is an easy method to assess a stock's value.

Sales per Share

My starting point is a ratio called 'sales per share'. It is calculated by dividing the sales for the last fiscal year by the number of issued common shares. For example, when I started to look at Fonorola (a company that I mentioned previously), its annual sales were $200 million. It had 10 million shares issued. Therefore, the sales per share ratio was $20 ($200 million ÷ 10 million). The reason I zero in on sales is that they demonstrate the strength of a company's products and services. Sales confirm that the general public is willing to part with their money to buy what the company has to offer. In my opinion, sales are one of the most unbiased measures of the economic value of the company.

Why do I find the sales per share ratio valuable? First, it provides me with a method to compare the cost of one company's share to the next. Second, I can also compare the sales per share to the market price (current price that the share is trading at on the stock market). This comparison helps me to judge if the share appears to be a bargain at the current price. Generally, I believe that there is value when the market price is less than the sales per share. For example, I bought Fonorola shares for the market price of $6, when its sales per share price was $20. I felt I had found a good deal.

The sales per share number is only a starting point. I also want to know how fast sales are growing. Rapid sales growth usually means that management has correctly predicted customers' needs, and has met them. I would pay more to own the shares of a company with rapid growth versus one with no growth at all. When I looked at Fonorola, the sales in 1992 were $43 million, 1993 - $60 million, 1994 - $108 million, and 1995 - $200 million. Such growth is remarkable.

It almost goes without saying that I am very reluctant to ever buy shares of any company that has no sales, (e.g. Bre-X). The fact is that one of the best ways to predict the future is to look at the past. I feel that a company with no sales has no verifiable proof that their management has been performing well.

<u>Earnings per Share</u>

But you may say, "What about the company's earnings? What good are sales if a company is not making a profit for the shareholders?" I agree, in the long run. However, in the short run, a corporation may be spending a huge sum on research (which will lower earnings), compared to an identical company that is spending nothing to develop future products. Thus, I find it difficult to judge a company's management by looking at its short-term profits. I want to know if management is doing the right thing in the long term. For example, at the time I bought Fonorola shares, the company was operating at a loss. From my discussions with the management, I found out that they were installing their own fiber optic telephone lines. Up to that time, they had been buying blocks of long distance service from Bell to resell to their own customers. I realized that once they had their own telephone lines, this huge drain of funds to Bell would be eliminated. I therefore had little concern that they were operating at a loss. Management had plans in place to make themselves very profitable in the very near future. That is exactly what happened.

There is another point I feel compelled to make. I previously mentioned that sometimes companies manipulate the sales figures in order to meet the month. However, short-term profits (earnings) are much more open to management interpretation than are sales. As an auditor, I am very skeptical about placing much confidence in the profit numbers reported.

Although I do not emphasize earnings per share in my analysis, I am nevertheless very interested in the company's long-term profitability. I must restate that in any company in which I invest, I already have confidence in their management, and therefore I know that they will be working hard to deliver earnings. I only invest in a corporation where top managers own a significant amount of the shares. Their interests are identical to mine i.e. long-term profits.

Book Value per Share

There's an important adjustment I make to the numbers that I use to find value. I subtract the 'book value' from the market price of the share that I am thinking of buying. Book value is the amount of money left to the shareholders if all operations ceased, assets were sold, and debts were paid. Dividing the book value by the number of shares issued gives you the 'book value per share'. (This number is usually calculated for you in the company's annual financial statements.) An investor expects to pay at least book value for a share because that is what the shareholders, as owners, could anticipate receiving if the company stopped operating. The way I see it, the book value portion of the amount I pay for a share is just an exchange of my cash for an equivalent value. The portion I pay over and above the book value is the only amount I am really paying to own the rights to future company profits.

Let's look closer at the Fonorola example. Their book value per share was $2.70 at the time I was looking into buying it. The share was trading at $6. Therefore, I was really only paying $3.30 ($6.00-$2.70) per share for sales of $20 per share. I would have been prepared to pay any amount up to the sales per share price of $20 to own this share!

Making the Decision

In expanding my search for Fonorola information, I contacted the company's investor service department. They answered some of my questions, and sent me an investor's information package. This package contained financial statements and positive research reports. It also gave the name and telephone number of the VP Finance, who invited investors with questions to call him directly. I did. I remember asking him why I should buy Fonorola shares versus those of their competitors. (Prior to calling, I had also studied the financial statements of the competitors.) From these discussions, I was even more convinced that Fonorola was well run. I then took the final step. I bought some of their stock.

I would like to share with you the process by which I selected another favorite company, Coca-Cola Beverages Limited (the Canadian operation of "The Coca-Cola Company", based in the U.S.). I had a friend who worked for them. He bragged that Coke Canada was the first beverage company in the world to be ISO 9000 certified. (This is an internationally accepted measure of quality control systems.) He therefore guaranteed me a terrific taste experience every time I had a can of Coke. He felt that their competitors could not match them. Coke had more hustle. When I queried him about why the company had not been rated as a star performer in the past few years, he pointed out that the present management had taken charge after that rating. They had since worked very hard to turn the company around. He was very confident in their ability.

There was one more factor that attracted me to Coca-Cola Beverages. The new managers were given a substantial number of share options. (An option is the right to buy a share at a predetermined price.) Options enable their owners to make a substantial amount of money if the share price rises. For example, imagine each key manager was given 10,000 share options at $8.00 each, when the share was trading at $7.00. Also assume that the share then goes up in value to $20.00. Each manager who cashes in his options at this time would make $120,000 ($20-$8=$12 x 10,000 options). If the share price does not go up, the options simply expire, as they always have time limits. Therefore, share options encourage management to work really hard so that the company's share price will go up.

At the time I was looking at Coca-Cola Beverages, their shares were trading at $7. The sales per share ratio was $20. I could not believe that I could buy a share of the world's most recognized brand name for only 35% of its sales per share. I considered this price such a steal that I did not even bother calculating and deducting the book value from the share price. I decided to add some of these shares to my portfolio.

About two and a half years later, the U.S. head office made a proposal to buy all the shares they did not already own for $22 per share. I was forced to sell, as over 98% of the other shareholders accepted this offer. The only reason that the head office bought all the outstanding shares of their Canadian operations was that they considered the cost of $22 per share to be undervalued. This shows what a great bargain it was at $7!

I want to emphasize that it was the quality, not the low price, which first attracted me to invest in Coca-Cola Beverages and Fonorola. Do not be tempted by what you think is a good price before you have done your research on the company. It is only occasionally that investment decisions are so obvious. It is therefore imperative to recognize and take advantage of such situations when they present themselves.

Borrowing to Invest

I believe your search for value is enhanced if you avoid borrowing to invest. As a personal example, two years ago I seriously thought about borrowing to buy shares that were trading at $12. I felt that this price was a bargain. I called a friend to ask his advice prior to my taking action. He strongly cautioned me against it, saying that borrowing to invest was synonymous with speculating. The dictionary defines speculating as "undertaking commercial transactions involving serious risk for the sake of possible large winnings."[24] I decided not to do it.

The temptation of timing and speculating is always there. I have to stand guard against it. I imagine a lot of other people have to do that, too. I am glad that I followed my friend's advice, but I had picked a winner, nevertheless. Today those shares are worth over $60. But the shares have gone down, as well as up, during the past two years.If I had taken out a large bank loan, would I have had the courage to hang on to the stock when its price was down?

Summary

I am always watching for new investment opportunities. My search for value starts with trying to assess the caliber and integrity of management. I want to tie my investment interests to a talented, hard working team. I want to know that this management team is capable, dedicated, and has a direct interest in making a lot of money for their corporation. Once I do find such a company, I try to assess how expensive the shares are relative to other opportunities. I do not invest in a company if I am not sure about it; I simply hold participation units (TIPS and SPYDERS) instead.

---

[24] The New Lexicon Webster's Dictionary of the English Language.

Chapter 14

Action Plan

"The golden age is not in the past, but in the future."

— E. H. Chapin

The financial data and advice available today is overwhelming. A lot of it is contradictory and confusing. It is difficult to make sense of it all.

So you want more money? Here's what works. Follow these five steps in the order that they appear.

The Simple Action Plan

1. Spend less than you earn.

2. Pay down debt.

3. Buy all the RRSPs you can afford up to your maximum and invest them in TIPS and DIA-MONDS.

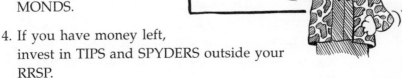

4. If you have money left, invest in TIPS and SPYDERS outside your RRSP.

5. Hang on.

The Simple Action Plan Expanded

Here is the simple plan with more detail. It is my opinion that if you follow this plan, you will break your dependency on a job. You will have enough money to 'retire'. And, there will be very few investors whose results will be better than yours.

1. Spend less than you earn.

Review Chapter 4, "Save Before Spending".

2. Pay down debt.

There is a big debate in financial planners' circles about whether it is better to first pay off debt, or buy RRSPs, if one cannot afford to do both. The answer is not perfectly obvious, so it does not matter a great deal. My personal preference is to put all extra money towards paying off debt first, because I have an aversion to debt. That is why I have put this as Step 2, but it really should be done in conjunction with Step 3.

You must pay taxes on any income that you earn. Only the after-tax money is available to pay off personal debt, such as credit cards, car loans, and mortgage. Once you have no debt payments, you will have a lot more money to invest or spend as you see fit. Therefore, one of the best steps you can take is to pay off all personal debt. This is one way of plugging leaks in your savings bucket.

3. Buy all the RRSPs you can afford up to your maximum, and invest them in TIPS and DIAMONDS.

Do not consider doing anything else until this goal has been accomplished. (I estimate that less than 5% of wage earners have managed to utilize all their RRSP room.)

There is no better investment than paying down debt and maximizing RRSPs. Financial planning is really that simple.

Open up a self-administered RRSP account at a discount broker, and keep all of your RRSP investments in that one spot. This will render your financial affairs as simple as possible. It is my experience that by simplifying your investments, you manage them better and your rate of return goes up. The bonus of this action is the decreased risk of any investments being misplaced. (I have seen it happen.)

At a discount broker, your fees for buying and selling securities will be as low as possible. This plugs one more leak in your savings bucket, and leaves you more money to be invested.

It is my expectation that equity investments (shares) will grow faster than cash investments (interest bearing). Participation units offer one of the most solid equity investment opportunities available. Therefore, I recommend that for your RRSP, you purchase participation units in this ratio: 80% TIPS and 20% DIAMONDS.[25] The 20% investment in DIAMONDS is the maximum foreign content that you are allowed in your RRSP account. (Historically, DIAMONDS have outperformed TIPS.) Note that foreign content rules are based on original cost. Therefore, if DIAMONDS appreciate faster than TIPS, you will still meet the foreign content regulations.

4. If you have money left, invest in TIPS and SPYDERS outside your RRSP.

·Once you have completed the steps of paying off debt and buying your maximum RRSPs, you can then start to make additional investments. To do this, I advise you to open up a second account (non-RRSP) at a discount broker. I recommend that you invest in TIPS and SPYDERS. As there are no foreign content limitations here, my suggestion

---

[25] Currently DIAMONDS are eligible as RRSP investments. If Revenue Canada rules that they are not eligible, invest in a low cost index fund that mimics the S&P 500 Index.

is to put as much as you feel comfortable with in SPYDERS, and then put the balance in TIPS.

5. Hang on.

Congratulations! You have just implemented an excellent investment strategy. The seedlings have been planted. Now be patient and let these investments grow.

Super Growth

TIPS, SPYDERS and DIAMONDS represent the market average. Can you beat their rates of return i.e. can you generate super growth? Yes – it is reasonable to assume that if you have done your homework, you <u>can</u> pick out companies that will perform better than the average.

The crux of super growth, however, is that you must diversify less. Also, be <u>very</u> familiar with the few companies in which you do invest. For example, Bill Gates, the world's wealthiest person, has many shares of Microsoft, a company that he knows very well!

SUPER GROWTH

Action Plan Results

The graph below compares the results of four different investment strategies (interest, TIPS, SPYDERS, and super growth). For each strategy, an investment of $1000 was made on January 1, 1992, and it was left untouched until June 30, 1998. The super growth results used in the graph represent my own investments.

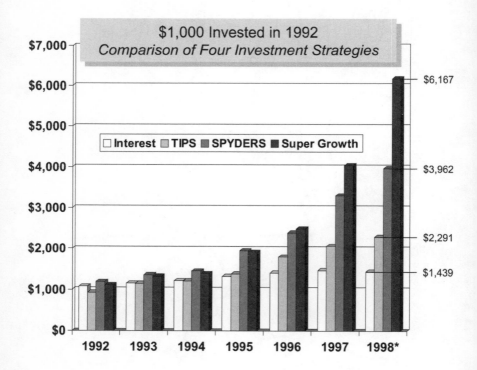

As you can see, there was a huge difference in the rates of return. The interest grew to $1,439, TIPS grew to $2,291, SPYDERS grew to $3,962, and super growth grew to $6,167. It is clear that while interest growth was steady, its performance paled when compared to the other more volatile options. However, TIPS lost money in 1992, which demonstrates that the results from equity investments are not always wonderful. Also note that this graph ignores taxes. Of the four options, the worst performer (interest) has the most punitive tax consequences.

Chapter 15

Children

Many people have a problem living within their means. Teach your children at an early age to spend less than they earn. Show them that invest- ing can be as exciting as

spending, and lead by example. There is no better financial gift that you can give them. It will last a lifetime.

An excellent way to interest your child in investing is to buy your child shares of a company. Since your child is a minor, the shares must be bought 'in trust' for him. This can be accomplished in two different ways - formal and infor- mal trusts. A formal trust is a legal agreement.[26] The tax laws, however, are a little gray in this area. I chose this sim- pler informal trust route i.e. I bought the shares for my chil- dren without going through the legal agreement process.

My favorite company share to buy for children is Wrigley Gum. (I bought one share for each of my three sons when they were young.) When the share is purchased, you will pay a brokerage fee, which will be out of proportion to the amount of the investment. That is not important. It <u>is</u> important to take delivery of this share, instead of having

---

[26] A trust requires the three certainties of intention, property and beneficiary. It should name the beneficiary (the person who receives the benefit - the shares), the settlor (the person who gives the shares), and the trustee (the person in charge of the trust). The trustee and the settlor should not be the same person. Also, it would be helpful if the trust document indicates that the share will not revert to the settlor, and that the settlor's permission is not required to distribute the share(s) to the beneficiary (the child).

the brokerage firm hold it for you. This way Wrigley has a record of you as a shareholder. (This is not the case if the brokerage firm holds the share for your child.) The actual share certificate, along with some forms, will be sent to you by mail. You will be asked if you wish to subscribe to the dividend reinvestment plan (DRIP). Mark the card "Yes" and return it. This means that you are allowed to buy more shares directly from the company, without paying commission. Also, dividends will be reinvested into more stock. These features, as nice as they are, are not why I want you to subscribe to the dividend reinvestment plan. The main reason is the educational value. Every Christmas, Wrigley will send your child a package containing 10 packs of gum. Your child will ask, "Why am I getting this gum, Mom or Dad?" You will answer "Because you are a shareholder." The child will then ask, "What is a shareholder?" This is a perfect opportunity to explain to him what he is able to understand.

SHARES FOR CHILDREN

The important point is that your child will be excited about investing. He will have experienced the rewards of investing in shares at a young age. This will have a very positive impact. I know that my three boys were certainly happy to get their Wrigley's gum for Christmas. This 'return' was very real for them, and it established their investment desire. (Years later, my oldest son Chris went one step further by investing his summer earnings in Wrigley's.)

Once their curiosity is aroused, take home The Globe and Mail, or another business paper, to show your children how to read the financial pages. Show them the current trading value of the stock that is invested for them. They may wish to monitor the share price as it goes up and down. It is their money that they are watching. There is no better opportunity to hook your children's interest in saving.

When Jon, my second-oldest child, was in grade eight, he chose to do a project on stocks, bonds and mutual funds. This, in turn, sparked the interest of Kevin, his eight-year-old brother. Kevin soon became very keen on the stock market, and asked me to sell him 50 Fonorola shares. I transferred these to him from my holdings. Every night, he eagerly waited for me to come home with the Globe and Mail so that he could check his stock. He was thrilled when the price of his stock doubled. It was really rewarding to see him studying the paper and reading the financial pages. Sometime later, he pretended that he had purchased certain shares, and he got great delight in watching how his imaginary portfolio was doing.

A year ago, Kevin asked me if he should spend his money on a Game Boy, or on more Fonorola shares. I told him it was a decision that only he could make. He ended up buying some shares in an American company called Electronic Arts. (This company makes most of his favorite computer games.) He already realizes that there are choices available to him, and that each choice has its consequences.

Once your children are interested in stocks, go to a brokerage house and open a separate trust account for each child. If grandparents or others wish to invest in the child's future, have them put money into the trust account, and use it to buy more shares. Every month, the brokerage firm will send a statement. It will list the company name, number of shares owned, their cost and their current market value. The brokerage firms (discount or full service) do all the book-keeping for you. If your child wants to buy a share with his own savings, do so in the same brokerage account. For his own information, record how many shares he bought himself.

Education is a major expense. It is prudent to plan and start saving early. Registered Education Savings Plans (RESPs) offer help in this area. The government contributes an additional 20% to the amount you have placed in the plan (up to an annual maximum of $400 per child). There are very few restrictions as to the type of investment that the plan may purchase. When funds are withdrawn for post-secondary education, the interest and income earned by the plan is taxed in the hands of the child. There are penalties if the RESP funds are used for anything other than the child's education.

Instead of using an RESP, you could buy shares and place them in the child's trust account. If your child decides not to pursue post secondary education, these savings may be used to assist her in starting a business or buying a house.

I favor the shares of companies that reinvest their earnings (instead of paying out the earnings as dividends), because their share price should increase more rapidly. When the shares are sold, the increase in value from their cost will be reflected as a capital gain. Income on capital gains is taxed in the hands of the child, for whom the funds are in trust. This is a big tax break, as the child's tax rate will always be less than that of the parent. If the funds are used for education, it is highly probable that the child won't have much income. As well, he will receive a tax deduction for tuition. Therefore, it is unlikely that he will owe any income tax. Interest and dividends, on the other hand, are taxed in the hands of the parent who gave these funds to the child. This is another reason why I like shares that do not pay out dividends.

Chapter 16

Conclusion

Not that long ago, a courageous young man named Terry Fox decided to run across Canada. The fact that he had an artificial leg did not deter him. He ran from St. John's,
Newfoundland to Thunder Bay, Ontario before succumbing to cancer. This was an amazing athletic feat. He captured our hearts with his dauntless determination to achieve his goal. Terry demonstrated that it is possible to accomplish almost anything if you want it badly enough. Likewise, if you want more money, you must be motivated.

There is an ancient legend that demonstrates the power of compound interest. A man named Sissa Ben Dahir invented the game of chess. For his efforts, he requested a reward. He asked King Shirham of India for what appeared would be a modest amount - the proceeds from a game that used simple mathematics. A grain of wheat was to be placed on the first square of the chessboard. The amount placed on the next square was always double the previous square, until all sixty-four squares were filled (i.e. 2, 4, 8, 16, 32, 64, 128, 256, etc). The total reward amounted to four trillion bushels, the world's wheat production for two thousand years! The moral of the story is that by saving and investing sensibly, a small amount of money will grow to a very large amount over time.

Buying an RRSP enables you, in effect, to double the money that you have invested. This is the same as moving one square ahead on the chessboard. The way to continue the momentum is to earn more money from the investment. How well the investment performs will determine how long it takes to once again double your money. You will be able to move ahead much faster if you choose equity rather than cash investments. Time is limited – use it wisely.

The legend clearly demonstrates that eventually investment growth will outstrip your spending desires. At this point, financial matters will no longer be of concern to you. However, don't confuse wealth with happiness. We are much wealthier today than any of our ancestors were. Yet we are not always happy, and it seems reasonable to assume that our ancestors were not always glum. Money in itself does not appear to solve our problems.

So you want more money? Combine your desire with the knowledge and skills you have learned from this book. Start now to spend less than you earn, and invest it wisely. The attainment of your goal is almost inevitable.

Chapter 17

Questions and Answers

The following are questions that I have been asked repeatedly. Perhaps you have wondered about the same things.

1. You have used a 10% rate of return for many of the examples in your book. How can I be assured of getting this rate of return for my investments?

I have been advising that you invest in TIPS and SPY-DERS. When you purchase these, it is different from locking in your money at a definite rate as you would with cash investments such as GICs and term deposits. However, the rate of return on SPYDERS for 1997 was 34%. Even though this rate is not guaranteed, I am very confident that it will continue to do well over the long run. Right now, the best rate you can hope for on a cash investment is about 5%.

2. Do you need a lot of income to become wealthy?

It is logical to assume that the more income you have, the more you can save and invest in order to become wealthy. However, this is not always the case. Some people with very high incomes feel very poor, and may in fact be worried about making their next mortgage payment! They have often formed the habit of spending all that they earn. Others, with much less annual income, have become very wealthy. Seems hard to believe, doesn't it?

3. I have trouble saving money. What can I do?

You are probably not aware of all the 'leaks' in your 'savings bucket'. Step one is to develop your feedback system. Once you know where your money is being spent, find creative ways to cut back. Carefully plan all purchases, and do comparative shopping. Carry less money with you to avoid impulse buying.

Many times, the only reason that people stop spending is that they have nothing left in their bank account. Don't rely on your banker to stop your expenditures. Instead of being a 'drifter', choose to be a 'decider'. Take control of your own spending.

4. Should I lease or buy a car?

Leasing is popular because it allows you to drive a new vehicle even if you do not have much money. However, you will be paying the leasing company for the service of both providing you with the car, and guaranteeing to buy back the car at the end of the lease. You will be money ahead by owning, instead of leasing.

Remember that if you are going to own a car, you would save even more money if you bought a good used car, instead of a brand new one.

5. How do I choose a financial advisor?

As I have indicated in the book, I feel that with some work, you can be your own best financial advisor. However, if you are determined to hire one, ask him some questions before doing so. If he will be handling your financial affairs, you want to be sure that he does a good job of handling his own financial affairs. First, ask him what his personal overall rate of return was for each of the last five years. If the advisor does not have a five-year track record, or does not know what his own rate of return was, you should be wary.

If his own rate of return was less than the S&P 500, why pay for his services when you could simply buy SPYDERS? Second, is his personal investment portfolio larger than yours? Why seek investment advice from someone who has less invested than you do? Third, how is his personal portfolio invested? Does he follow his own advice? This speaks volumes. You want to work with an honest and open person who will share this information with you.

Finally, ask how the financial advisor is paid. A straight fee for service is preferable to an indirect fee, which is earned by someone getting paid a commission for selling you mutual funds. Also, check what would happen if you want to sell these investments. Are there any hidden charges or trailer fees? It is best to avoid these.

6. What does "the magic of compound growth" mean?

An investor receives interest from an investment. This interest is added back to the base amount, and now the investor is earning money on the original investment plus the interest. This process keeps happening over time. Thus, interest is being earned on an ever-increasing base. Results can be remarkable. The mutual fund charts, often seen in advertising, reflect compound growth.

At 10% annual growth, money doubles every 7.2 years.[27] Compound growth is very powerful. Review the charts in the appendix to see its impact.

If you do not pay off credit card balances in full every month, then the magic of compound growth is working for the banks - not you! The typical rate of interest

---

[27] To easily calculate how many years it takes to double an investment, divide the interest rate into 72.

charged on credit cards is 17½%. If you have a balance owing of $500, and you never pay anything off, then in four years you will owe the bank $1000. Mortgages are also based on compounding interest, so imagine how much you can save by paying your mortgage off early.

7. Must I set up a special savings fund for my child's education?

No, it is not necessary to earmark a separate fund for education, but it may encourage you to save. I like RESPs. However, an advantage to saving outside an RESP is that if the money is not used for education, it can be used to help your child make a down payment on a house, start her own business, or take a vacation. The point is to always have some money squirreled away, so that you have no financial worries, and can help your child reach her dreams.

8. If I do set up an RESP for my child's education, what should I invest it in?

My first recommendation would be to invest it in SPY-DERS. It has a great track record, and it is in U.S. dollars. This helps if your child will be attending an American college. My second choice would be to invest it in TIPS.

9. Would the age of my child make any difference in the types of investments that I hold in her RESP?

You should only be concerned about holding investments that, in the long run, have the least risk and the highest rate of return. Therefore, the age of your child is not important.

10. My mother is 65 and a widow. She has only a small pension and very little savings. What can she do to secure her financial future?

Unfortunately, there is not much that can be done now. It is too late to start talking about investments, as all her money is required for her living expenses.

Archimedes, a great Greek mathematician and physicist, once said, "Give me a fulcrum and a lever long enough, and I will move the world." In her case, the 'long enough' time element is missing.

11. My mother is 65, a widow and has about $500,000 in term deposits. She does not really need this money, because she has enough pension money to live on. Should this money be invested differently?

Whether your mother invests differently or not, it would appear that she has sufficient money to meet her needs. If I was in her shoes, there is no doubt that I would invest it all in TIPS and SPYDERS. Historically, equity investments such as these have had a higher rate of return than cash investments. However, it is important that your mother be comfortable with her portfolio. Because she is used to interest bearing investments, she may get nervous if she switches to participation units, and they go up or down in value.

Her money will likely pass to the next generation, or even to her grandchildren. When this happens, will it be spent immediately, or will it continue to be invested? The length of time that this money stays invested could be significant, so this would be another reason to lean towards equity.

12. I am 25, and have $10,000 in my RRSPs. I know nothing about the stock market. How would you recommend I invest this money?

Open a self-administered RRSP, and invest it in TIPS. As you find out more about the stock market, you may wish to invest in a specific company if one really impresses you. However, do your research on this company before switching out of participation units.

13. I don't have much money. Can I go to a broker to invest it and not be embarrassed?

Try not to worry about having only a little money as you start out. The important point is that you are saving. Anyway, if you use a discount broker, all your transactions are handled over the telephone. The only time you will meet a person face to face is when you open the account.

Having said that, it would be best if you could accumulate about $500 prior to investing. There is a transaction fee of about $30 every time you buy or sell stocks, so investing this amount will make it worth your while.

14. I do not have your contacts or experience. How can I determine the quality of a company to invest in?

Rely on your experience with the companies around you. First, look at the company where you work, assuming that its shares are traded on the stock exchange. Second, be observant when you deal with any other company. Are you 'wowed' by the experience, or glad that it is over? Are its products and service excellent and consistent? Is it busy? Is it expanding? As a consumer, you are in a good position to monitor a company's quality.

However, remember that until you find a company that impresses you, keep your money in participation units (TIPS and SPYDERS).

15. As a new investor, I feel that I could choose a mutual fund more easily than a specific stock.

At the end of 1991, there were about 500 Canadian mutual funds. This number doubled to about 1,000 by 1997. There are currently fewer than 1,400 companies listed on the Toronto Stock Exchange. Soon the number of mutual funds will exceed the number of companies listed on the exchange. Therefore, it is just as difficult to pick a good mutual fund as it is to pick a good stock.

The only reason the number of mutual funds has doubled in the past six years, is that the mutual fund companies have found them to be very profitable. In many cases, investors would have made a lot more money by buying the shares of the mutual fund company itself, rather than the mutual fund products that they sold!

If you want to own a 'mutual fund', simply buy participation units.

16. How do I know if my investments are doing well?

I compare my year-to-date growth results to that of the S&P 500 index for my U.S. investments, and the TSE 35 index for my Canadian investments. These benchmark numbers are readily available from financial newspapers, radio, television, and the Internet.

17. If TIPS and SPYDERS are such good investments, why have I never heard about them before?

Businesses prosper by marketing products on which they make money. There are no commissions paid for selling participation units, so they are generally not promoted.

The more something is pushed, the more cautious one should be. Do not confuse advertising with value. Perhaps the opposite is true. TIPS and SPYDERS have outperformed most highly advertised investment products.

18. It is very easy to buy RRSP mutual funds. I have money deducted from my pay, and the mutual funds are bought for me. Can I buy TIPS for my RRSP in the same way?

Yes. The first step is to open up a self-administered RRSP account at a financial institution such as a bank. The second step is to have a portion of your pay direct deposited to this new self-administered account. This is really no change from what you have been doing. The third step is to buy TIPS with the money that is now 'inside' (and keeps accumulating in) your new RRSP account. This is a matter of picking up the phone, and placing the order. I would also transfer all your other RRSP holdings to this one account, so that they are all in the same place.

It will cost you a minimum of $30 in brokerage fees every time you purchase TIPS. Therefore, to save money you may wish to place a purchase order either once a quarter, semi-annually, or annually.

19. I have GICs in my RRSP. When they come due, can I buy shares with this money?

There are several steps involved, but it can be done. Again you must first open a self-administered RRSP plan, because this is the only RRSP account that permits you to hold shares. When your GIC matures, transfer the money from it directly to the account you just opened. (Do not withdraw the funds from your RRSP, or you will pay taxes on it.) Now that your GIC money is in your self-administered account, buy shares.

20. Could another stock market crash, such as the one that happened in 1929, occur again?

This may be the question that I am asked most frequently. I cannot guarantee that a similar stock market crash will never occur again. I also cannot guarantee that the airplane you plan to take will not crash. That does not mean you should never fly.

We, as humans, tend to put too much emphasis on large and/or emotionally charged events, and too little emphasis on smaller ones. Your concern about the 1929 stock crash is a reflection of probability blindness. As I have said before, in the long run stocks have provided the best return on investment when compared to all other options.

21. If stock prices are down, is it a good time to buy?

Your question is really one about market timing. I do not try to time the market. I simply want to buy a stock whenever I have the money to invest. However, the best time to buy is when the market is down, because you do get more shares for your money.

22. Why did you not include derivatives as an investment option?

Derivatives are financial instruments that derive their value from some underlying interest such as an equity, debt, currency, or commodity. These financial instruments are complex. I do not touch them, and I feel they are not appropriate for the average investor. My philosophy is to go directly to share ownership.

23. I have heard stories about people losing their equity investments by trusting someone who seems totally honest. How can I protect myself?

One way to protect yourself is to be certain that your shares are held in trust for you. Brokerage firms do this. Even if the brokerage firm goes under, the shares are still yours. Giving your money and investments to someone who seems honest, but does not hold them in trust for you, is risky. Never buy shares from telephone solicitors.

HEY, C'MON! TRUST ME.

Also, be informed. You should always know exactly how much you have invested, and in what.

24. I like cash investments. How can I have them all in one account, if I have more than the CDIC insurance limit of $60,000?

If you hold a lot of cash investments, it is very easy to have one account and still have the entire amount protected. You can accomplish this by purchasing government bonds. No matter what amount is invested in these, they automatically carry the government guarantee.

25. Are financial institutions immune from failure?

No, they are not. In Gordon Pape's book "Building Wealth", he points out that the following financial institutions had to be bailed out by the CDIC after they fell on rough times:

Astra Trust, Pioneer Trust, Commonwealth Trust, Security Trust, London Loan, District Trust, Fidelity Trust, Western Capital Trust, Northguard Mortgage Corporation, Northland Bank, Canadian Commercial Bank, Standard Trust, Shoppers Trust, First City Trust, Bank of Credit and Commerce International, and Saskatchewan Trust.

26. I feel that my wealth is not real until I sell my shares to get cash.

You are stating that, in your opinion, only cash is real. In fact, neither cash nor shares are real. Cash is simply ink on paper. A share is also ink on paper. It is the idea of what the ink represents that we accept as important. You would feel rich if this ink indicated that you had a million dollars. The key factor to consider is the purchasing power represented. A thousand dollars in shares can purchase the same amount of goods as a thousand dollars in cash.

The other idea central to this question is that the value of the stock may go down just before you sell. This is true. Share prices are very unpredictable in the short term, but they are very predictable over the long term.

Glossary

Bank Reconciliation: the process of comparing your recorded bank transactions e.g. your chequebook, to the bank's records e.g. the bank statement, in order to find any discrepancies in either, and then correct them.

Bond: a type of debt instrument used by corporations and governments to fund their cash requirements. They are usually sold in denominations of $1,000 (their face value), have a coupon (interest rate) fixed to the face value, and a maturity date (when the interest stops and you can cash in the bond). A bond can be bought or sold in the bond market, so that you can receive cash for it without waiting until the bond matures.

Book Value: the net worth of a corporation (common stock plus retained earnings). Book value is an approximation of its break up value. This is the amount that would be left to distribute to the common shareholders, if all operations ceased and assets were sold for their recorded values.

Book Value Per Share: the book value of the corporation divided by the number of shares issued.

Broker: a person who is paid a fee to buy or sell stocks, bonds, and other securities. This name is interchangeable with stockbroker.

Brokerage House: a corporation that specializes in buying and selling stocks, bonds, and related securities. Brokers work for a brokerage house.

Canada Deposit Insurance Corporation (CDIC): provides insurance for cash and cash investments at banks and trust companies. It is limited to $60,000 per investor at each financial institution.

Capital Gain: the profit that results from selling investments such as stocks or bonds. Another way to understand capital gains is to think of an apple tree. The apples produced each year are income. The growth of the tree, from the time you plant it to the time you sell it, represents a capital gain.

Cash Investments: when you lend your money for a period of time, in exchange for a fee (the interest paid to you). Examples include savings accounts, bonds, Canada Savings Bonds, GICs, and term deposits.

Compound Interest: when interest is earned not only on the initial principal, but also on the accumulated interest of prior periods. Compound interest is contrasted to simple interest, which is earned on just the principal.

Corporation: a legal entity that has many of the same rights as a person. For example, it can own property, run a business, enter into contracts, hire, and pay people. It provides a way for investors to pool their money, and start a business that is separate from them.

Diamonds: a participation unit, trading on the American Stock Exchange, that reflects the Dow Jones Industrial Average. Its stock symbol is DIA.

Dividend: a distribution of a corporation's retained earnings to its shareholders.

Earnings Per Share: the annual after tax earnings of a corporation, divided by the number of shares outstanding.

Equity: another term for a share. It is also used to describe the net worth of a business.

Guaranteed Investment Certificate (GIC): a common type of bank deposit. Your money is usually locked in for terms of one to three years.

Index: a specific group of stocks used by investors as a market benchmark. Examples include the Dow Jones Industrial Average, S&P 500, and TSE 35.

Liquidity: the ease of exchanging an asset for cash. All other things being equal, liquid assets (easily convertible to cash) are preferred to less liquid ones.

Mutual Fund: an investment fund that issues shares on a continuous basis. Money is invested in a large pool with other investors. These shares may be redeemed at any time for their underlying asset value.

Over-The-Counter Markets: all facilities that provide for security transactions not conducted on organized exchanges.

Participation Unit: a basket of stocks held in trust. It reflects a stock market index, and trades like a share.

Price/Earnings Ratio: the ratio of the stock price to the earnings per share.

Retained Earnings: after tax profits that are retained in the business, rather than paid out as dividends.

Return On Investment (ROI): the amount of money the investment earns in a year, divided by the original amount of the investment.

RRIF: Registered Retirement Income Fund. At age 69, funds from an RRSP must be transferred to a RRIF. It is similar to an RRSP, with the difference being that a specified amount of money must be withdrawn from a RRIF each year.

RRSP: Registered Retirement Savings Plan. A government sponsored plan that provides tax advantages to encourage saving for retirement. No taxes are paid on money put into the plan, or its earnings, until the funds are withdrawn.

Share: ownership of part of a corporation, i.e. its equity. The term is interchangeable with common share and stock.

SPYDERS: a participation unit, trading on the American Stock Exchange, that reflects the Standard and Poors 500 Index (S&P 500). Its stock symbol is SPY.

Stock: another name for a share.

Stock Exchange: a place where stocks, bonds and other securities are bought and sold. It is really an association of stockbrokers, who meet together (now by computer) to buy and sell securities, according to fixed regulations.

Stock Split: an accounting transaction, whereby the number of shares of a corporation is increased. For example, in a 2-for-1 stock split, each share becomes two, but the shareholder's portion of corporation ownership does not change.

Term Deposit: similar to a GIC i.e. money is deposited in a financial institution for a period of time. Term deposits are usually not as long term as GICs.

TIPS 35: a participation unit, trading on the Toronto Stock Exchange, that reflects the Toronto 35 index. Its stock symbol is TIP.

Appendix

Results of Non RRSP Investing

The table below shows what an investment of $6.50 per day will grow to at various interest rates. This money is not invested in an RRSP.[28]

YEAR	8%	10%	12%	18%
1	2,370	2,370	2,370	2,370
2	4,852	4,880	4,908	4,992
3	7,451	7,538	7,625	7,892
4	10,173	10,352	10,535	11,100
5	13,023	13,333	13,651	14,649
6	16,007	16,490	16,988	18,574
7	19,133	19,833	20,560	22,917
8	22,406	23,373	24,386	27,721
9	25,834	27,122	28,482	33,035
10	29,423	31,092	32,869	38,913
11	33,182	35,297	37,566	45,416
12	37,118	39,749	42,596	52,609
13	41,240	44,464	47,982	60,566
14	45,556	49,458	53,749	69,368
15	50,077	54,746	59,924	79,105
16	54,810	60,346	66,537	89,876
17	59,767	66,276	73,617	101,791
18	64,958	72,556	81,200	114,971
19	70,394	79,207	89,319	129,551
20	76,087	86,250	98,012	145,679

---

[28] A tax rate of 41% was assumed for the calculation of taxes on interest earned. There is no more tax owing on amounts shown.

YEAR	8%	10%	12%	18%
21	82,048	93,709	107,322	163,520
22	88,291	101,608	117,290	183,256
23	94,828	109,973	127,964	205,087
24	101,674	118,831	139,394	229,238
25	108,843	128,212	151,633	255,953
26	116,350	138,147	164,739	285,505
27	124,212	148,668	178,772	318,196
28	132,445	159,809	193,799	354,358
29	141,066	171,608	209,890	394,361
30	150,095	184,103	227,120	438,612
31	159,549	197,335	245,570	487,563
32	169,450	211,347	265,327	541,712
33	179,818	226,187	286,482	601,612
34	190,675	241,902	309,135	667,873
35	202,045	258,544	333,392	741,171
36	213,952	276,168	359,366	822,253
37	226,420	294,832	387,179	911,946
38	239,477	314,597	416,961	1,011,165
39	253,151	335,528	448,852	1,120,921
40	267,469	357,695	483,001	1,242,333

Results of RRSP Investing

The table below shows what an investment of $6.50 per day will grow to at various interest rates. This money is invested in an RRSP.[29]

YEAR	8%	10%	12%	18%
1	4,000	4,000	4,000	4,000
2	8,320	8,400	8,480	8,720
3	12,986	13,240	13,498	14,290
4	18,024	18,564	19,117	20,862
5	23,466	24,420	25,411	28,617
6	29,344	30,862	32,461	37,768
7	35,691	37,949	40,356	48,566
8	42,547	45,744	49,199	61,308
9	49,950	54,318	59,103	76,343
10	57,946	63,750	70,195	94,085
11	66,582	74,125	82,618	115,021
12	75,909	85,537	96,533	139,724
13	85,981	98,091	112,116	168,875
14	96,860	111,900	129,570	203,272
15	108,608	127,090	149,119	243,861
16	121,297	143,799	171,013	291,756
17	135,001	162,179	195,535	348,272
18	149,801	182,397	222,999	414,961
19	165,785	204,636	253,759	493,654
20	183,048	229,100	288,210	586,512

---

[29] A tax rate of 41% was assumed on RRSPs purchased, and this saving was added to the RRSP investment. When withdrawn, taxes are owing on the amounts shown.

YEAR	8%	10%	12%	18%
21	201,692	256,010	326,795	696,084
22	221,827	285,611	370,010	825,379
23	243,573	318,172	418,412	977,947
24	267,059	353,989	472,621	1,157,978
25	292,424	393,388	533,335	1,370,414
26	319,818	436,727	601,336	1,621,088
27	349,403	484,400	677,496	1,916,884
28	381,355	536,840	762,796	2,265,924
29	415,864	594,524	858,331	2,677,790
30	453,133	657,976	965,331	3,163,792
31	493,383	727,774	1,085,170	3,737,275
32	536,854	804,551	1,219,391	4,413,984
33	583,802	889,006	1,369,718	5,212,501
34	634,507	981,907	1,538,084	6,154,751
35	689,267	1,084,097	1,726,654	7,266,606
36	748,409	1,196,507	1,937,852	8,578,596
37	812,281	1,320,158	1,937,852	10,126,743
38	881,264	1,456,174	2,174,395	11,953,557
39	955,765	1,605,791	2,439,322	14,109,197
40	1,036,226	1,770,370	2,736,041	16,652,852